DAN ARCHER

Harry Oakes

DORIS ARCHER

Gwen Berryman

The Archers

THE NEW OFFICIAL COMPANION

Borchester Echo

PRICE 6d.   AND FELPERSHAM GAZETTE   DECEMBER, 1959

AMBRIDGE WOMAN ACCUSED IN GEMS CASE

Port and airfield watch for Madame Garonne

By Our Own Correspondent

Madame Garonne (extreme left) with Mr. Grenville at a church fete— a picture taken in the early autumn.

SENSATIONAL allegations in a French daily newspaper have linked the name of Madame Denise Garonne, housekeeper to Mr. Charles Grenville, of Ambridge, with an international ring of diamond smugglers. Madame Garonne, who recently disappeared from the village under mysterious circumstances, is one of fifteen people accused by ex-Sûreté detective, Vincent Pichou, in a frank, hard-hitting interview published in " L'Etoile de Marseilles."

Monsieur Pichou has spent the past five years as a private investigator with the South African Diamond Corporation. He has been solely engaged in combating the smuggling of industrial diamonds from Africa to Amsterdam.

Since the war the problem of smuggling from the diamond fields has grown so acute that millions of pounds worth of stones are now lost annually.

Most of the investigations have been carried out by Interpol. Monsieur Pichou is quoted as saying: "It is they who have discovered the information implicating a number of prominent and outwardly respectable people.

Confessions

"Nine out of fifteen diamond smugglers have already been arrested. Two have made detailed confessions, naming accomplices."

Among those unmasked, Monsieur Pichou alleges, is Madame Garonne, whom he describes as "an ultra-smart divorcee, who acquired a cloak of respectability by attaching herself at the end of 1945 to the household of an English diplomat in the British Colonial Service, Mr. Charles Grenville."

"L'Etoile" goes on to state that Interpol have issued a warrant for the arrest of Madame Garonne, but that she has disappeared from an English village near Borchester, where she has been mixing in local society since last March.

Rooms searched

Information has now reached "The Borchester Echo" that shortly after Madame Garonne's departure, Mr. Grenville was visited by a Scotland Yard detective who conducted an examination of her living quarters.

We have also been informed that ports and airfields are being watched by police who wish to question her.

Mr. Grenville refused to discuss Madame Garonne with our reporter. His only comment was: "I know nothing about this. Surely it's utter nonsense?"

Threatened closure of Borchester Market

"IF BORCHESTER MARKET is closed, we should make it our duty to boycott the town." This was the opinion of Mr. Herbert Toombs, of Woodford Farm, Penny Hassett, expressed at a special meeting of the Borchester branch of the National Farmers' Union called to discuss the future of Borchester Cattle Market.

The meeting followed a letter from Mr John Harris (clerk to the Council) stating that in its present position the market was a great hindrance to the development of the centre of the town. The letter went on to state that the rates and tolls bore no relationship to the potential value of the site.

There were two suggestions put forward for discussion by the meeting:

1. Should the market be closed as unnecessary?
2. Should it be rebuilt on a site on the outskirts of the town?

Mr. Toombs thought the whole project was short-sighted.

300 years

As far as he knew, the market had been in existence for more than three hundred years, bringing business to the shopkeepers and tradesmen throughout its history.

But if the council wanted to adopt a "get rich quick" policy by fostering more industry in the town, then country people should boycott Borchester and take their business elsewhere.

'Sound scheme'

Mr. Philip Archer, of Ambridge, thought that Mr. Toombs was exaggerating the position, and that a new market on the outskirts of the town would be a sound scheme, easing the traffic problem on market days.

Mr. Archer added: " If the council would be prepared to build an abattoir as part of the proposed new market then local butchers would be more inclined to purchase their requirements locally. This, of course, would help to build up the market."

After much discussion it was suggested that the Vice Chairman and the Secretary should seek a meeting with the Markets Committee of the council, and the auctioneers concerned with the market, and report back with more detailed information at the next meeting.

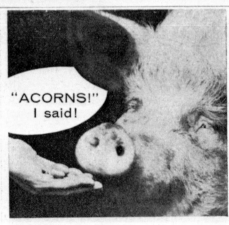

The Archers

THE NEW OFFICIAL COMPANION

A toast to celebrate the 2000th episode. Thelma Rodgers (Peggy), Lesley Saweard (Christine), Ysanne Churchman (Grace), Norman Painting (Phil), Patricia Greene (Jill).

William Smethurst

WEIDENFELD AND NICOLSON · LONDON

By arrangement with the British Broadcasting Corporation

Published in Great Britain by
George Weidenfeld & Nicolson Limited
91 Clapham High Street
London SW4 7TA

ISBN 0 297 792 008

Printed in Great Britain by
Butler & Tanner Ltd, Frome and London

Designed by Gaye Allen

The publishers are grateful to the following for permission to
use photographs:

BBC Enterprises: ii, 7, 8, 14 above, 16, 17, 18 above, 19, 21, 22, 23, 26, 27, 30, 36,
37 right, 38, 39, 40, 41, 42, 45 below, 46 above, 48, 49, 51, 66, 70, 72, 73 above,
96 above, 112. Birmingham Post and Mail: 6, 11 below, 115 left. Camera Press:
10. Daily Telegraph Colour Library (photographer Chris Cheetham): colour page
8. Alan Dudley:
114. Express Newspapers: 101 above. Heart of England Newspapers Ltd: 12
above. Radio Times Hulton Picture Library: 29, 73 below.

The map on pages 88–9 and on the back jacket: Illustration ©
Robert Jones, BBC. Licensed by BBC Enterprises Ltd
Published by David & Charles Publishers and available as a
folded map $6\frac{3}{4} \times 5$ in.

Half title: Walter's 90th Birthday Party, 1986 – and Mrs Perkins
is the guest of honour!

Facing title page: From the *Daily Sketch*, February 1959.

Contents

1
The Archers

'The most enduringly successful programme of its kind'

The first meeting between producer (Tony Shryane) and cast, 1951.

The longest-running daily serial in the world, The Archers will be thirty-seven years old in January 1988.

The programme has long been a gatherer of curious facts and statistics. When it was twenty-five somebody worked out that 20,000 cups of tea had been poured and consumed in the farm kitchens of Ambridge, and that the Brookfield cows had been milked 26,000 times. When the programme was thirty the press was eager to report that 20 million words had been spoken since The Archers started.

There are, however, one or two facts about the programme that can be claimed with complete confidence. UK transmissions are heard by a growing and devoted following in Holland, Belgium and Northern France. (The growing popularity on the continent came to light when the *International Herald Tribune* ran a major article on the programme, claiming that to listen to The Archers was by far and away the most chic thing for anyone to do in Paris these days!); and around the world, events in Ambridge are followed via the British Forces Broadcasting Service.

The programme goes out twice a day from Cologne, Gibraltar, Malta and Cyprus, and is somehow overheard by a surprising number of listeners in Israel. However, there is an unfortunate gap for much of the Middle East, and you cannot hear The Archers at all in Central Asia, Afghanistan or Iran – a deprivation that might account for the troubled history of that region in recent years.

Then, more happily, we come to Nepal, Malaya, Borneo and Hong Kong (very good Archers country) – and over the blue Pacific to Belize in Latin America.

The newest station of all is The Falklands, where the daily stories of Walter and Mrs P, of Phil and Jill, and Elizabeth and David, of Sid Perks and Kathy Holland, and all the other inhabitants of England's most famous village, are now beamed out over the South Atlantic to the puzzled penguins and no doubt irritated Argentinians.

The Archers is, perhaps, the last vestige of Empire; the programme on which the sun never sets. 'As o'er each continent and island, the dawn brings in another

Early days in the Broad Street, Birmingham, studios. Harry Oakes recording with Gwen Berryman.

The original writing team in 1954: Geoffrey Webb and Edward J. Mason.

day' – well, it does so to the sound of Barwick Green, the famous signature tune that is heard (statistics again) forty-eight times, every twenty-four hours, as the earth turns.

'Dallas' can certainly do better. So, perhaps, can 'Coronation Street'. But it is a remarkable achievement for a modest, low-budget radio programme that started life as an advisory service to small-scale farmers in the English Midlands.

Let us delve back for a moment into pre-history. Not quite to the Ice Age and the Ichthyosaurus, but to the days when Britain had only one television channel, which operated for only a few hours each evening, and on which the 'Adventures of Muffin the Mule' were watched on murky, flickering, 14-inch black-and-white sets. Radio reigned supreme! The nation was gripped by the 'Billy Cotton Band Show', 'Have a Go' with Wilfred Pickles, and by the amazing 'Adventures of PC49'.

The idea for The Archers came up at a meeting between farmers, the BBC and the government. Farmers were not modernising as fast as the Ministry of Agriculture believed they ought to have been doing. They were not enthusiastic about herbicides, and pesticides, and artificial fertilisers. They were not – and this was the crucial point – *listening* as often as they might to the BBC's farming advisory

programmes. How could they be persuaded to listen, eagerly, and with undivided attention? That was the question under debate, and at some point a Lincolnshire farmer made a spontaneous, off-the-cuff remark: 'What we need,' he said, 'is a farming Dick Barton' – and we are told that everyone in the conference *laughed*. And so they might have done because 'Dick Barton – Special Agent', with his fearless aides Jock and Snowy whizzed round the world getting into amazingly desperate situations and then wriggling out of them. Dick Barton was as remote from a BBC advisory programme on farming practice as you could get.

It was ridiculous. But – as in so many ridiculous soap-opera plots – it happened. A BBC producer at the meeting, Godfrey Baseley, who was to become The Archers' first editor, wrote later: 'I began to think of the excitement that could develop from an agricultural story: the cow that lost her calf; the sugarbeet crop that failed; the importance of the Ministry of Agriculture's February Price Review . . .'

And the Lincolnshire farmer, Mr Henry Burtt of Dowsby, explained himself: 'I've a hundred acres of blackcurrants, and if I were to find blackbud rearing its ugly head among those acres of bushes I would be as horrified as Dick Barton if he found himself in a pit full of crocodiles.'

Around the world television networks are full of creative teams eagerly seeking the magic formula for the next major 'soap'. They want a show that will attract vast audiences, sell in a hundred different countries, and run for ever! The doctor's surgery – the hotel – the business empire – the downmarket back-street – the newspaper. Should it be sex and glamour or a simple tale of family life? Should it be romantic and escapist, or gritty and real? What is the flavour of the year in this most competitive and cut-throat section of the entertainment industry?

I wonder how many programme directors would jump out of their chairs with joy shouting 'Eureka!' or 'That's the one!' if a writer or researcher said: 'Let's do a major soap about blackcurrants and the February Price Review!'

And yet, after thirty-seven years, The Archers remains the only surviving major radio serial in the English language!

The formula was irresistible. What listeners to the BBC's light programme wanted was a story of ploughmen homeward plodding their weary way and

Norman Painting joins the cast as Phil Archer.

lowing herds winding slowly o'er the lea. They wanted to hear about the Archer family, cosy round the tea-table at Brookfield Farm eating Doris Archer's apple cakes and free-range boiled eggs. They wanted to hear nineteen-year-old milk sampler Christine pronounce on the latest Milk Marketing Board hygiene regulations, while 21-year-old Philip pondered over *The Pig-breeder's Weekly* and Dan Archer read aloud (and quite slowly) extracts from the latest Ministry of Agriculture hand-out on the eradication of the warble fly.

That was what The Archers was supposedly all about. Real people in real situations, coping with the real problems of life.

The trouble is that if you examine the stories which ran in the first year or so, a picture emerges of something quite different. It is a picture not of homely rural joys but of sex, and violence, of romance and adventure. In the first twelve months our young earnest pig-breeder Phil was knocked unconscious after leaping on to the running board of his girl-friend's car as she sped away, crazed with jealousy after seeing him in the passionate embrace of a willowy, blonde, poultry-farm assistant. His girl-friend, Grace, then fell madly in love with the neurotic, war-wounded victim of Korea, Lt. Alan Carey.

And Phil's sister, milk-recordist Christine, had love affairs with three men in rapid succession before developing a very strange friendship indeed with a certain Lady Hydleberrow, who hated seeing her with boys and wanted to take her away to Ethiopia. (Wise old Dan forbad the trip and compensated her with a job looking after the chickens at Brookfield.)

Elsewhere in the village Phil's sister-in-law, Peggy, was fending off the passionate advances of Jack's business partner, Barney Lee; people were hit over the head by saboteurs plotting to wreck an ironstone drilling site; a shifty character called Bill Slater was killed in a fight outside The Bull public house; and an Irish thriller writer was exposed as something quite different – not, as the village had been led to expect, the embezzling Major Smith of the Pay Corps, but as secret-service agent Mike Daly MC who was hiding under an assumed identity in order to confuse the King's enemies.

An everyday story of countryfolk? Villages of the English shires may have their fair share of excitement. But they rarely have so much, so fast.

Recording a 'musical evening at Brookfield', 1954.

In its early days, The Archers was a combination of 'Dallas', 'Dynasty', and rather blatent agricultural propaganda. And it was phenomenally successful. Two million listeners in the first week, four million by the end of the first month, and by 1955 an incredible 20 million. Every night half the adult population of Britain was tuning in to hear about Phil's love life and about jet planes crashing on the village, about masked raiders hitting old ladies over the head, about spies and diamond smugglers, and about the high milk yields possible from Friesian cows fed on high-protein concentrates.

Britain was a highly industrialised country. But the propaganda of The Archers was so successful that what the population didn't know about high-yielding Friesian cows, or the life cycle of the warble fly, wasn't worth knowing.

The formula worked – and it went on working for some fifteen years. Then, some time in the late Sixties, things began to go wrong. There was a brilliantly successful story about Jennifer's illegitimate baby, Adam; then a couple of years later an appalling and embarrassing story about little Adam being kidnapped. It wasn't that the listeners didn't care about little Adam, it was just that they didn't believe it. Godfrey Baseley, the man who had fought so hard to get the programme off the ground, and who had devised most of the characters and invented most of the early stories, found himself presiding over a programme that no longer worked and that was losing its audience at an alarming rate. New formulas were drawn up. Plans for the Seventies were worked out. A desperate scheme to imitate the plots and stories in television's 'The Forsythe Saga' was put forward. The growth of television was blamed and Godfrey Baseley bluntly refused to allow Dan to get a set at Brookfield on the grounds that every viewer gained by BBC TV was a listener lost to him. But it was not only the lure of television that was costing the programme dear. It was poor characterisation, poor stories, and creaking dialogue.

In 1970 came the first warning memo from programme heads in London:

That we are in trouble is now becoming very obvious to our most loyal and keen listeners, particularly those who have always appreciated the accuracy and authenticity of the programme. If this situation is allowed to go on for much longer I shall find it very difficult to justify the programme as 'a reflection of the social and economic life of the countryside' when I talk to the BBC Agricultural Advisory Committee.

The Archers was tired. In 1968 almost 80 per cent of listeners believed it was true to life. By 1971 less than 60 per cent believed in it. Over a supposedly casual lunch in London, the Head of Network Radio in Birmingham, Jock Gallagher, was told that he had only 'a few months' to put the programme right, or it would be taken off the air.

Jock Gallagher, Head of Network Radio, Pebble Mill.

A clutch of Cambridge curates come to Pebble Mill to meet their favourite barmaid Caroline Bone (Sara Coward).

Above: Norman Painting and Arnold Peters sign autographs at the Town and Country Festival, 1984.

There were few in those dark, desolate days, who would have predicted that fifteen years later the Controller of Radio 4 would write: 'In the face of terrifying competition, its profile and reputation have never been higher,' while *The Listener* would say: 'Still the Ambridge myth endures, sustained by some of the best acting, direction and writing on radio,' and the January 1986 edition of *Marxism Today* would report: 'Suddenly the Archers have become fashionable,' and worry about *why* through several thousand words.

'There seems to be an amalgam of "young fogeyish" nostalgia and radical chic about admitting that one actually listens to the programme,' wrote a puzzled *Marxism Today*. 'Characters in The Archers seem somehow to be deeply ingrained in our collective folk memory, they inhabit that twilight world where you are never really sure whether they do exist or not ...'

And *The Listener* even warned that the programme was getting too successful for its own good:

> The basic problem, I suspect, may be one of increased self-consciousness. The programme-makers *know* that The Archers is a national institution, listened to by the great and the good and even the Royal, as well as some four million others – the most enduringly successful programme of its kind. They know that it is increasingly popular among younger listeners (bucking the Radio 4 trend) and among the AB socio-economic groups (50% of the audience now as against 40% ten years ago). It is not surprising that, with all the indicators set fair, the temptation is to raise the profile higher and higher ...

Today newspaper was also concerned by The Archers' new-found success, and summed up the current plot-line in an attempt to fathom the mystery:

> In Denver there were two Krystle Carringtons, one kidnapped and one with a permanent headache to fend off husband Blake. In Dallas they were still mourning Bobby Ewing's death. In Ambridge, Jethro Larkin had his dog's photograph taken in a booth in Borchester and Mrs Antrobus became editor of the parish magazine.

Left: A new Clarrie – Fiona Mathieson joins the programme to play opposite Trevor Harrison.

Today then went on to report:

Six years ago, the average Archers' fan was a woman over 50, who thought Shula Archer was a young tearaway. Now the latest goings-on in Ambridge are discussed by bright young things at posh dinner parties – perhaps the poshest, since the Queen, the Queen Mother and the Princess of Wales are known to be fans. At *The Times* there is talk of forming a Nelson Gabriel fan club.

The transformation in the programme's fortunes has been remarkable. And most of the credit must go to a man who has remained firmly in the background through the long years of revival, whose picture never appears in the papers, and whose name is seldom mentioned. Jock Gallagher, the man given 'a few months' to sort things out in 1971 has overseen its development ever since. To him fell the task of replacing Godfrey Baseley (who had no desire at all to go, and for long made bad-tempered sniping noises from his home, named Ambridge, deep in rural Gloucestershire) and bringing in Malcolm Lynch, the script editor of 'Coronation Street'. And when Malcolm's health gave way under the strain, Jock moved in and edited the programme himself before the appointment of the veteran radio-drama producer, Charles Lefeaux, who was to guide the programme with a cool nerve and steady hand until his retirement in 1978. Jock, though, was the man with final responsibility. Through almost half the programme's long history he has guarded it from attack, represented it to higher authority, appointed key staff to work on it, and given decisive and pungent advice about the serial's characters, writers, and the abilities of individual actors. If this guidance has sometimes been less than gratefully received (the wise radio producer at Pebble Mill knows that if he can't stand up to Jock he's had it) Jock has the great, and within the media at least, rare, virtue of remaining steadfastly loyal to those who work for him.

And what of the future? Jock Gallagher is still in

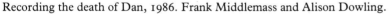

Recording the death of Dan, 1986. Frank Middlemass and Alison Dowling.

Above: Script meetings are held every month at Pebble Mill.

Below: Glenys Kinnock – an avid Archers listener – was guest of honour at the 35th anniversary celebrations, January 1986. Sarah Fellowes (Production Secretary), Dick Francis (Managing Director, Radio), Ronnie Henry (Production Secretary), William Smethurst (Editor), Glenys Kinnock.

charge of the programme he was given 'a few months' to rescue back in 1971, and in the editor's chair is former agricultural journalist Liz Rigbey, a long-time follower of the programme whose episodes have now been going out for over a year, and whose warmth of personality, and sheer capacity for hard work have impressed everyone on the team.

'As Ambridge enters the late 80s what have we to look forward to?' asked *Marxism Today* after its long analysis of the programme's success.

Will Mark Hebden break the hegemony of the Conservatives as the automatic choice of the new Archer generation? Will the character of Hazel Woolley, who has been so closely modelled on Joan Collins in 'Dynasty' that one can almost hear the shoulder pads, be brought out again to expose an unknown element of the past of an important member of the Ambridge community? Or will Shane the silent, shadowy and possibly gay barman in Nelson Gabriel's wine bar suddenly come to the fore to provide the swelling number of Archer fans with a real taste of soap?

These are questions to which only Jock Gallagher and Liz Rigbey know the answer!

35th Anniversary Photograph, 1986: *Front row (left to right)*: Hedli Niklaus, Heather Barrett, Fiona Mathieson, Alison Dowling, Charlotte Martin; *2nd row:* Norman Painting, George Hart, Bob Arnold, Chriss Gittins, Pauline Seville, June Spencer; *3rd row:* Pat Gallimore, Terry Molloy, Colin Skipp, Mollie Harris, Richard Derrington, Patricia Greene, Brian Hewlett, Jack May, Angela Piper; *Back row:* Ted Moult, Trevor Harrison, David Vann, Alan Devereux, Arnold Peters.

2

The Ambridge Story 1951-60

Dan's trusty worker Simon (*right*) shows asthmatic Londoner Bill Slater how to operate the new Brookfield tractor. Slater was Peggy's cousin, but Dan found him a bad worker. John Franklyn (Bill), Eddie Robinson (Simon).

1951

Dan Archer, tenant of 100-acre Brookfield Farm, sadly retired his two faithful old shire horses, Blossom and Boxer, and bought a tractor. In the summer he was made Vice-President of Ambridge Tennis Club and took his wife Doris for a week's holiday to Aberystwyth.

Phil Archer's girlfriend Grace Fairbrother fell in love with Korean War veteran Lt. Alan Carey so Phil had a tempestuous romance with blonde, blue-eyed Jane Maxwell.

Three million tons of ironstone deposits were found on the Fairbrothers' land, and mysterious saboteurs tried to stop drilling.

A son was born to Peggy and Jack Archer, and they called him Anthony William Daniel. Peggy's mother, Mrs Perkins, moved to Ambridge from the East End of London. She brought a great deal of furniture with her. Peggy's cousin, Bill Slater, was killed in a drunken brawl outside The Bull and subsequently revealed as the mining saboteur!

Nelson Gabriel was promoted to Corporal in the RAF.

Grace found Phil kissing Jane Maxwell late at night in the farm office. Phil chased after Grace, jumped on to the running board of her car, hit his head on a tree branch, and was knocked unconscious. When he recovered Grace proposed to him, but he confessed to a fatal infatuation with Jane.

Jack Archer gave up his smallholding and chrysanthemum business and went to join his wartime chum Barney Lee on a farm in Cornwall.

Jack Archer was serving in the army when he met pretty ATS girl Peggy Perkins, who said she was a socialist. After the War they married and returned to Ambridge, where Jack struggled with potted chrysanths on his smallholding. Denis Folwell (Jack).

1952

A turbulent year for young Christine Archer, who worked as a milk tester for Borchester Dairies. She called off her romance with *Borchester Echo* reporter Dick Raymond, and Dick went off to Malaya to 'try to forget'. Christine became friendly with a mysterious Lady Hydleberrow who insisted on calling her 'Felicity', hated her going out with boys, and tried to take her off on a trip to Ethiopia. Dan firmly opposed the idea. Christine gave up her job at Borchester Dairies and came home to look after the chickens at Brookfield.

Phil started going out with Grace again. In the spring he overturned his tractor on Lakey Hill. He had an eye operation and Grace cried a lot. He said he would marry her when he had saved £2,000. Grace said she had no intention of waiting five years and stormed off.

Peggy and the children (Jennifer who was six, Lilian who was four, and baby Anthony William Daniel) went to join Jack in Cornwall, but the whole family returned after Jack's partner Barney Lee made lecherous advances to Peggy.

Above: Christine helps her mum with the washing up. After a heady romance with reporter Dick Raymond she gave up her job and helped Dan with the Brookfield poultry. Pamela Mant (Christine), Gwen Berryman (Doris).

Below: Cleaning out the cowshed. In 1952 Dan sold his six cows giving low-fat milk and bought two prize shorthorns for 100 guineas each. Harry Oakes (Dan).

Point-to-point rider Reggie Trentham married Valerie Grayson (a former secret service agent) and they began to run Grey Gables Country Club.

Doris was nominated as President of Ambridge WI. She was horrified when people accused her of buying votes by giving away bottled gooseberries and plums.

Dan bought Christine a horse called Midnight, and Walter Gabriel tried without success to make a television set for Mrs Perkins.

Peggy and Jack applied for the licence of The Bull. At the end of the year Peggy was ill with diphtheria and taken to Felpersham Isolation Hospital.

1953

The Squire's nephew, Clive Lawson-Hope, came to Ambridge to reorganise his uncle's estate. He took Grace to the pictures in Borchester, kissed her in his motor car, then asked her to marry him. She asked for time to think. While she was doing so Clive went off the idea.

Peggy came out of hospital and was shocked by rumours that Jack was having an affair with schoolmistress Elsie Catcher.

Walter held a Coronation Party at his run-down farm. Mrs Perkins bought a television set to watch the great event.

On Coronation Eve Phil and Grace were back together again – roasting potatoes at the Lakey Hill bonfire until four in the morning. Then Grace decided to go to Ireland for a year and they quarrelled at her farewell party.

Walter Gabriel's sheep were attacked by dogs, and Nelson was taken seriously ill. Walter had to rush to Southampton RAF hospital to give him blood.

A newcomer to the village was John Tregorran, a 'bearded wanderer with a green caravan,' who suddenly appeared on Heydon Berrow. He was soon revealed as a university lecturer who had won £12,000 on the pools, and he opted for a life of rural romance. Jack was highly suspicious and accused him of stealing The Bull's Christmas Club money. When gypsies stole one of Christine's horses John went after them and recovered it. On Christmas Eve the gypsies set fire to his green caravan.

Above: Dan in the sitting room at Brookfield, 1953. To mark the 'New Elizabethan' age he grew lucerne and tried his hand at making silage.

Below: After his (rumoured) affair with Elsie Catcher, Jack casts an appreciative eye over Peggy. In the summer of 1953 she was forced to take over as licencee of The Bull after the brewery complained about Jack. Thelma Rogers (Peggy).

1954

The Squire's unscrupulous nephew, Clive Lawson-Hope, started to escort lovely young Christine Archer to the pictures and kissed her in his motor car. Everyone was surprised when he offered to marry her, and even more surprised when she turned him down. He went off to his Uncle Percy's farm in Africa.

A smartly dressed young lady from Surrey called Carol Grey bought Jack's old smallholding. Soon after her arrival she drove round a bend and knocked John Tregorran off his scooter.

A young, dashing horse-owner called Paul Johnson asked Christine to ride for him at a two-day show at Belverton.

Peggy insisted that Jack see a doctor because of his erratic behaviour and vile temper. The doctor admitted him to the county hospital for mental disorders.

Squire Lawson-Hope sold the estate, and Dan bought Brookfield Farm.

Phil moved his pig-breeding scheme to Coombe Farm and Grace sent him a set of fishing rods for his birthday. In the autumn she came home from Ireland. Phil proposed to her and she said 'yes'.

Irish thriller-writer and secret service agent Mike Daley bought seventy acres of woodland from the Squire then went on a mysterious venture with a lady called Baroness Czorva. Neither of them were ever seen again.

John Tregorran found Christine alone at Brookfield and kissed her. Then he proposed to Carol Grey – she did not reply.

Opposite left: Christine plays with a kitten and wonders whether or not to marry Clive Lawson-Hope. Phil objected because Clive was a cad, and Squire Lawson-Hope objected because Christine was the daughter of a tenant. Dan left her to make up her own mind. Lesley Saweard (Christine).

Right: Business deals in the city for Mr Fairbrother. He was delighted when Grace announced her engagement to his young farm manager Phil Archer, and offered them Coombe Farm at a rent of £1 a week. Leslie Bowmar (Mr Fairbrother).

1955

Squire Lawson-Hope held a shoot for his former tenants, then sadly left Ambridge. Gamekeeper Tom Forrest was given a pension of £1 a week for the rest of his life.

Phil and Grace were married on Easter Monday. Jack was best man and Christine was a bridesmaid.

Christine passed her scooter test and started to go round with Paul Johnson and his horse-owning set.

Riding a fiery mare belonging to Reggie Trentham she suffered a fall and broke her collar-bone. When she recovered, Paul and Reggie whisked her off to a race meeting at Scowell Braddon. Dan reproved her for going about with racy types.

John Tregorran spent the summer organising a village 'Make Merry Fair' and declaring his love for Carol Grey. When she entertained Reggie Trentham until 1 a.m. he shouted at her, and when he called to shout at her again she wouldn't let him in.

Doris laid a crazy-paving path round her garden. Myxomatosis reached Ambridge and wiped out the rabbits eating Dan's corn.

Phil was offered a directorship by Mr Fairbrother. During a celebration dinner at Grey Gables a fire broke out in the stables. Grace was injured by a falling beam while rescuing Midnight. She died in Phil's arms on the way to hospital.

Dan reproves Christine for going about with racy types, and tells her she's just the daughter of a humble tenant farmer.

Carol Grey dusts a photograph of her jealous admirer, John Tregorran. Anne Cullen (Carol), Basil Jones (John).

Walter presents a prize cauliflower to Mrs Perkins, but she is not impressed. In the summer of 1955 farmer Joe Blower bought a motor car and started taking her out for joy rides. Chriss Gittins (Walter), Pauline Seville (Mrs Perkins).

1956

Foot-and-mouth disease broke out at Brookfield, and all the stock was slaughtered. PC Brydon stood guard at the farm gate to stop anyone entering or leaving. Farmhands Len Thomas and Simon dug a pit to bury the carcasses.

Christine went into partnership at the stables with Paul Johnson's sister, Sally. In June Paul proposed to her and she accepted.

At Brookfield Doris painted the kitchen scarlet and grey, and Dan thought of retiring.

The village baker, Doughy Hood, claimed that John Tregorran was a villain and not to be trusted. He refused to say why for several weeks. It then emerged that a man called Ron Tregorran had swindled Doughy's friend out of a lot of money.

Fairbrother confiscated ten acres of Walter Gabriel's farm and gave them to Phil to grow blackcurrants on.

Fairbrother gave Phil a cine camera and advised him to start a village cine club, which he did. On 15 December Christine married Paul. She wore a white lace dress with paper taffeta petticoats, and Doris wore an empire-line dress of purple silk. Phil filmed the wedding with his cine camera.

Coffee break at the riding stables, and Christine had plenty of gossip for Sally Johnson and Maggie Hood. No sooner had she become engaged to Paul than Nelson Gabriel had come home on leave and tried to kiss her. When she said she was promised to another he said he didn't care! Anne Chatterley (Sally), Jean Lester (Maggie).

Life was full of pain and drudgery for Walter Gabriel. In 1956 his new landlord, George Fairbrother, confiscated 10 acres of his 40-acre farm and gave them to Phil. Walter said he would give up farming next Lady Day.

1957

Walter gave up farming. He bought a minibus and was granted a haulage and carrier's licence.

Phil met Jill Patterson – an attractive girl with blonde, urchin-cut hair, wearing a yellow dress – at the village fête. A few weeks later he proposed to her at New Street Station, Birmingham. She asked for time to think.

Farmhand Ned Larkin's unmarried brother, Bob, followed him to Ambridge and made eyes at Pru Harris, the barmaid at The Bull. Tom Forrest (who was courting Pru very slowly) was incensed. One night he struggled with a poacher in the woods and shot him dead. It was Bob Larkin. At Gloucester Assizes Tom was acquitted of manslaughter. The Borchester silver band welcomed him back to Ambridge.

Dan's brother Frank died in New Zealand, and his widow Laura came to live in Ambridge. Doris said she must always regard Brookfield as her home.

On the second anniversary of Grace's death, Phil took Jill Patterson to the churchyard and they put flowers on her grave. Phil again proposed to Jill, and this time was accepted. They married quietly at Crudley Church on 16 November.

Aunt Laura had a heart attack while visiting her friend Nellie MacDonald in Stourhampton.

Above: A new career for Walter Gabriel! He began a carrier service to Borchester and Mrs P gave him a spotlight for his birthday. Then teddy boys stole his bus from outside the village hall and slashed the seats.

Below: Tea-time at Brookfield. In the summer of 1957 Phil met Jill Patterson while he was filming the Ambridge Fête (opened by Humphrey Lyttleton), and a few weeks later he proposed. Norman Painting (Phil).

1958

Little Lilian Archer went skating on the village pond and fell through the ice. She was rescued by her father and Ned Larkin.

Tom Forrest agonised for months about Pru Harris, his black-eyed barmaid from The Bull. In the end he proposed, was accepted, and they married on 26 September.

Walter disappeared from Ambridge. On his return he admitted that he had been forced to go and clear Nelson's debts. He cheered himself up by blowing a hunting horn loudly through the Ambridge–Penny Hassett cricket match.

John Tregorran took over the village cine club from Phil, and asked Doris to help him organise a folk music club. Doris was delighted.

Jill gave birth to twins – and Dan was very surprised to find he had grandchildren called Shula and Kenton.

The Squire's wife Lettie Lawson-Hope died. In her will she left Glebe Cottage and four acres of woodland to Doris for her lifetime. Dan tracked down old Blossom and Boxer, and Lettie's coffin was pulled to church on a haywagon.

Pru Forrest was X-rayed by a mobile chest unit and a dark patch was revealed on her lung. She was sent to a sanatorium for several months.

Happy days for Doris. Her brother Tom was about to be married, daughter-in-law Jill was pregnant, and she herself was busy organising a folk music club with John Tregorran.

1959

The Fairbrothers moved abroad and businessman Charles Grenville bought the Ambridge Estate. Stourhampton Brewery offered to sell The Bull to Peggy and Jack for £5,300. Aunt Laura gave them most of the money to buy it.

Thieves stole a biscuit tin of money from Walter's cottage. The money was recovered by John Tregorran and PC Brydon, who trapped a gypsy in Arkwright Hall. On a further visit to Arkwright Hall (ghost hunting with Ned Larkin) John Tregorran found a hoard of gold sovereigns.

Mrs P. married her second Perkins – Arthur Perkins – and they went to live in London.

The Brookfield farm apprentice Jimmy Grange formed a skiffle group and Dan and Doris went to a concert in Borchester. Doris said that young people must be encouraged to do their best.

Above: Dan staggers under the weight of misfortunes. In 1958 blight ruined his potato crop, he lost his oats after a fire in the dutch barn, and six lambs were killed by lightning. Doris had all her teeth out. Arnold Peters (Len Thomas).

Below: Mrs P assures Walter it is better to have loved and lost, than never have loved at all. She was about to marry Arthur Perkins, who had come to Ambridge to work on a memorial window for Grace in St Stephen's Church. Walter was devastated.

A fond look from Doris as Dan rests from his labours. 1959 was unlucky for him: he fractured his leg, slipped off his crutches, and was sent to hospital in Oxford with suspected pneumothorax.

Pru returned to Ambridge, and a newcomer was Charles Grenville's mysterious and sophisticated housekeeper Madame Garonne. Later in the year Madame Garonne disappeared. She was exposed in the *Borchester Echo* as a notorious diamond smuggler.

Dan fell off the implement shed and was seriously injured. Returning home after several weeks in hospital he fell over in the dairy when his crutches slipped.

Jill gave birth to a son, David Thomas.

1960

Charles Grenville bought Arkwright Hall and gave it to the village as a community centre. Doris was appointed to the General Purposes Committee.

Fowl pest wiped out Dan's chickens. He gave up poultry and formed a milk co-operative with Fred Barratt and Jess Allard.

Walter felled a tree for his neighbour Mrs Turvey and it fell on her garden shed, smashing it to bits. Then he had smashed up his minibus and lost his school-bus contract.

Tom and Pru considered becoming foster parents. They visited a little boy called Johnny Martin in a children's home.

Paul Johnson and Phil went to Paris, where Paul encountered a girl called Marianne Peters. Later Marianne turned up in Borchester and began to meet Paul secretly. When Christine became suspicious he claimed that Marianne was the daughter of an old school friend, and that he was helping her to get a job. Christine was more suspicious than ever.

Phil and Grenville went to Holland on business, and Carol Grey travelled with them. Phil developed a poisoned foot and went into hospital. When Grenville and Carol visited him they announced that they were engaged to be married.

Bitter days for Walter Gabriel. Pining for Mrs P he smashed up both his mini bus and Mrs Turvey's shed. Eventually he started a pig venture with Ned Larkin.

Christine with her horse Midnight at Brookfield Farm. Chris had little to be cheerful about. Husband Paul had caught chicken-pox, lost four hounds while hunting the Ambridge pack, and was having a 'relationship' with a girl called Marianne.

Below: Jimmy Grange serenades the Brookfield pigs. When he came to Ambridge Jimmy borrowed Phil's cine camera and dropped it out of his bedroom window. Then he was accused of stealing youth club funds. Alan Rothwell (Jimmy Grange).

'Oh you mean, nasty, destructive creatures!'

Dear Sir,

Like Mrs. Snell whose letter in the Radio Times, 12-18 April I have just read, I too deplore the "leaks" which so often occur in the newspapers. Likewise, when I read a book I do not read the end, or the middle, but prefer to enjoy the story as it unfolds.

Sadly, I had not heard of this particular leak until I read Mrs. Snell's letter! Did you really have to print it!

To the Archers,

12.2.82.

Oh you mean, nasty, destructive creatures, to get rid for ever of the lovely, endearing, bright as a button, fresh as a daisy, true little English country Rose our beloved little Polly. How could you do such a nasty evil thing to one of its true country characters in its programme, I feel sad beyond measure, I feel that my enjoyment of the programme has been marred for ever and that you do not deserve a faithful following ever again. Why, Why, Why

Polly were al... ... the village after various misfortunes ...

No! – I am not prepared to accept an explanation that it was a lesson in road safety or actor resignation. I only hope that the scriptwriters will ... Archers 'afficionados' any further suffering ... ...laught... ...way to get over the trauma o... ...ew ha... marriag...

Dear Mr Perks.

Please accept my sadness on your sad passing off your good wife Polly. I still cannot take it in. many sad lives have been broken since the life of the Archers started. each week-day has be... a new chapter of life to w...

Having been an "Archers" fan for very many years, I am absolutely incensed at the way you "killed" off Polly.

February is a gloomy month anyway, & for the last few editions having to listen to the "acted" grief has been so painful I have been forced to turn it off, & I know I am not the only one.

'Smile at us, pay us, pass us;' wrote G. K. Chesterton, 'but do not quite forget; For we are the people of England, that never have spoken yet.'

They might not have spoken, but the people of England (and of Wales, but not, to any great extent, Scotland) have written a prodigious number of letters since The Archers began. 'Why, oh why,' they so often complain, 'can't it be like it used to be!' and the answer is, alas, that it never ever was like it used to be. The golden age for one listener will always be the age of irritation and disappointment for another.

Some letters come from worried listeners, concerned about the terrible effects that certain aspects in the programme might have on the public at large. 'In the episode when Myra came to dinner Dan was heard praising some sort of fig pudding,' worried Mr D. G. of Guildford:

> Now obviously your script writer does not wear dentures or he would have realised that figs in any form are impossible to eat with dentures because of the millions of tiny seeds. Dan is certain to have some false teeth and as he is over 80 it is more than likely that Phil is old enough to have had at least a part set of false teeth so Jill could have been expected to know about the agony of trying to eat figs with dentures.

Other letters beg for information. 'I am intrigued with the artificial insemination you have mentioned,' wrote a lady from Castle Bolton. 'Could you put me in the picture as to what it is and how you administer it? It sounds to me something false. I should be so pleased if you would improve my knowledge of this AI business.'

Such letters are all in a day's work for The Archers' editor. But there were some great issues – love, death, and sending Nigel Pargetter to Africa – that shook the nation to its core and prompted a deluge of mail. Back in 1953 it was the torrid romance between Phil and Grace.

'Take my advice and drop that nasty piece of work, Grace,' wrote a Peterborough listener, who firmly believed that Phil was a real person. 'Let that Clive Lawson-Hope have her … he'll have none of her rotten bursts of temper. Take off those blinkers, choose a wife who'll be a help mate, an even-tempered and industrious person with similar ideas to yourself.' And from Surrey came the good-natured missive: 'I am glad to hear you are going with Grace again and

that your pigs so far have not got swine fever. Hope you have a nice Coronation Day.' An eleven-year-old from Oxfordshire even penned a poem:

> Love is sweet
> But oh how bitter
> To love a girl
> And never get her.
> Now Grace lives over the sea,
> What a good swimmer you ought to be.

Listeners like a good romance. They write friendly, amusing, relaxed letters. When a love affair is in the offing they do not write bitterly or angrily, or demand that the editor be sacked. A death on the programme is quite a different matter.

'Oh you mean, nasty, destructive creatures!' wrote (or rather sobbed) a lady from King's Norton, Birmingham (an address dangerously close to the studio) in February 1982, 'to get rid for ever of the lovely, endearing, bright as a button, fresh as a daisy, true little English country Rose our beloved little Polly …'

And the postbag for the death of Polly Perks was indeed enormous. That huge but usually slumbering beast, Archers Public Opinion, had been roused. The deluge of mail and phone calls was greater than anything seen since the death of Grace in a stables fire twenty-nine years before.

'I am absolutely devastated at the dreadful happening you have brought into the above programme this evening. What a horrid thing to do. Is there not enough misery in this world today?'

'I am absolutely incensed at the way you killed off Polly. February is a gloomy month anyway and the last few editions have been so painful I have been forced to turn off …'

'No! I am not prepared to accept an explanation that it was a lesson in road safety …'

'Poor Polly Perks is the victim, the latest in a long line reaching back to Grace Archer. One only hopes the blood lust has been satisfied for another year.'

'Writing out Polly Perks was cruel. Will The Archers be better off without her? No, no, no. It would be better off without YOU.'

Only one letter adopted a helpful note: 'I don't remember hearing of a dog at The Bull, and thought public houses usually have at least one for protection. Could Sid or Lucy have a puppy to ease their loss?'

Several writers accepted the 'tragedy' as having

Tony gave the bride away and Jennifer was matron of honour when Lilian (*centre*) married Ralph Bellamy in 1971.

Doris Archer smiles happily as her grand-daughter marries the Squire of Ambridge.

Rehearsals for the Christmas Revue, 1980 – George, Neil, Eddie, Brian, Phil, Shula and Tom.

David and Elizabeth ponder by the cowsheds.

Eddie Grundy.

Tea-time at Brookfield.

Jack Woolley.

Elizabeth helps her mother prune the roses.

Tom shows his gun to Sophie.

Phil and Jethro.

Tom drops in for a natter.

Inspecting the Brookfield herd – Jethro, Brian and Phil.

Sid and Kathy outside The Bull.

BORCHESTER SKETCH

SHE'LL MAKE AMBRIDGE A

SCANDAL VILLAGE

TOUGH AT THE BULL

☆ Peggy Archer at work in the cellars of The Bull. It's a tough life for a woman, and the profits hardly make it worth while. But there's no security in husband Jack's job as a fruit foreman. And there's the future of their three children to think of.

SHOCKER plans to blast the secret scandals of Ambridge across the world are being made in London to-day.

Last night I discovered that 25-year-old Sheila Trevelyan has kept her threat.

She HAS written the book that Ambridge dreaded — a scorcher called Glasshouse Village.

Three months ago Miss Trevelyan—once a Fleet-street journalist—stormed out of Ambridge after her hopes of marriage were shattered.

Ten days after her engagement to John Tregorran—she caught him on the rebound—she was told it was all off.

So she swore that Ambridge would hear more of her—and regret having to do so.

And she made it clear that she would write a book based on Ambridge.

"I'll call it Glasshouse Village—for very obvious reasons," she told them.

Maybe you remember how she discussed the book with Tony Stobeman.

'Great joy'

He asked her if she was writing the book "to get her own back for the way she had been treated." Her reply: "Yes, with great joy."

Warnings of possible libel proceedings were laughed away.

"I can't say that worries me very much." she said.

It was on that note that she left—leaving Ambridge guessing and vaguely uneasy.

As weeks passed the threat of Glasshouse Village faded. Ambridge began to forget. . . .

Then last night came the news which stirs up the worry—and looks like churning up the mud.

In her Knightsbridge flat Miss Trevelyan announced that the book has been written.

"I've been working almost round the clock on it for the last 12 weeks," she said. "It is now in the hands of my publishers."

What does she reveal in it? What shocks are in store for Ambridge?

"Let's just say that it will shake quite a few people," she said. "At the moment I'd sooner not say any more."

Jilted Sheila plans revenge —in a book

By LESLIE WATKINS

Joan Hood proposes!

Borchester Sketch Reporter
JOAN HOOD astounded Jimmy Grange last night BY PROPOSING MARRIAGE.

And he astounded her BY FIRMLY REJECTING HER.

"You are not bulldozing me into an early marriage with umpteen kids," he said.

"I don't want to marry anyone for ten years."

But Joan wouldn't be turned down so easily. "I'll wait ten years," she said.

And that was almost the last straw for Jimmy. He didn't stop to think before blurting out his answer:

"But hang it all Joan —where's your pride? I might meet someone else and fall in love."

Then Joan really showed the other side of her character—the tough go-getting side.

"You'd better not," she warned. "I can be horrid when I like. . . ."

★ See Dorothy Hart's advice to Joan Hood on Page 12.

IS THIS THE JOB FOR A WOMAN?

Borchester Sketch Reporter
THIRTY - SHIL-LINGS clear profit was made in The Bull this week. Not enough to buy a bottle of Scotch—or a coat for one of the kids.

Yet, to earn that money, 35 - year - old Peggy Archer has been forcing herself to work a 15-hour day. She starts before 6.30 a.m. and finishes about 11.30 p.m.

Security

Why does she do it? Is it worth while?

The obvious answer is Certainly Not. She should get rid of her licence — start enjoying life.

But there's another more important answer which is not quite so obvious. . . .

Peggy is not just a working mum straining for the luxuries of life. She is straining for security—for herself, her husband, her three children.

Consider the case-history of the Jack Archer family.

Peggy has never found much financial security in the marriage. There's always been that element of doubt and worry.

For Jack is basically unstable. He seemed to forget that he had to support three children—Jennifer, who is now 14, Lillian, 12, and Anthony William, eight.

He was too ready to squander his money, to go off on heavy drinking sessions with "the boys."

Then came his mental breakdown. It took him to hospital for six months.

In those six months Peggy had to fight on alone . . . and became

Fifteen hours a day—for 30 shillings profit

the licensee of The Bull. To-day Jack has a steady job . . . earning £12 a week as fruit foreman on the Fairbrother Estate.

But this is the niggling question:

How long will it last?

When the new boss—Oliver Charles Grenville—takes over the estate he may well fire Jack.

Pioneer

For Grenville is a pioneering type — the type who would realise the developing importance of fruit, who may want to expand production.

And, he may well feel that Jack—with comparatively little experience and no technical training—is not the man to have charge of a new, large project.

So Peggy is clinging to The Bull as a sheet anchor.

"After all, things aren't often as bad as this week," she said last night, "In the summer—what with people dropping in for meals—I can make a steady £8 or £9 a week, and there have been times when it's been £15 a week.

"And, you never know, there may be a time when you really need that money."

That's as much as Peggy is prepared to admit. But I suspect there's another thought

also behind her determination.

Jack seems to be settling down—and yet there is always a chance that the past will repeat itself.

That, I feel, is what Peggy is fighting to guard against.

Crash

Another woman with almost a parallel problem is Helen Fairbrother.

Life was smooth and unruffled for her—until the big crash. Fairbrother's serious illness knocked him out of action.

And suddenly Helen found her rôle had changed completely. She could no longer be just the pleasant little wife jogging placidly along in her husband's shadow. She had to take over — start running his affairs.

Certainly she's had some criticism over some of her methods. But no one can deny that she's done her best—and will have to continue doing so for a long time.

Breakers move on Tom's home

DEMOLITION teams will soon be moving in on Tom Forrest.

By the time his wife Prue is ready to leave the sanatorium for the cottage—there may be no cottage.

For the building is

doomed. It's due to be smashed out of the way to clear the route for the new road round Ambridge.

"What those planning blokes will never understand is that this isn't just another cottage to me," said Tom last night.

"This is home to me. Always has been.

"And what about my dog-pens and bird-runs? I couldn't go shifting all them." Plans are under way for the Forrest family to move into a new home one day.

The Daily Sketch, 6 February 1959.

been real. One sent £5 for a wreath (and then phoned to check on the kind of flowers it contained), and another wrote: 'Please accept my sadness on the passing of your good wife Polly. I still cannot take it in. Many sad lives have been broken since the life of The Archers started . . .'

But if there is one thing that enrages the Archers' correspondent more than a death, it is knowing about it beforehand. News that Polly was to be killed in a road accident was leaked to the press a week before it happened on air. Most correspondents believed the leak was a deliberate publicity stunt.

'How ironic! All last week I was mentally congratulating the BBC and the press for not commenting on the death of Dan Archer. Then what happens? He doesn't, after all, die at all, and instead we are given prior warning that Polly Perks will die! Please try to stop this publicity! Surely surprise and suspense are what make a serial?'

'There's no need to listen to the Archers anymore for I can hear all about it in the papers. Why spoil our listening by telling us about Polly beforehand?'

When Dan did, finally, suffer a fatal heart attack the story yet again was leaked a fortnight before it happened on air, and a Mrs Snell wrote bitterly to *Radio Times* complaining about it, and *Radio Times* printed the letter and roused a tide of indignation:

'Like Mrs Snell I too deplore the "leaks" which spoil my listening of The Archers. Sadly, I had not heard of this particular leak until I read Mrs Snell's letter. Did you really have to print it?'

And a sixteen-year-old from Burntwood, Staffs, wrote in similar vein: 'After reading the letter from Mrs Jane Snell, Dorset, in this week's *Radio Times*

I was most angry. Does she not realise that had she not written the letter other regular listeners and myself would know nothing about such statements? I would like to point out to her that not everyone receives a paper!'

Another correspondent pointed out that leaks only featured in what he called the 'comics' and called for a mass switch to the *Daily Telegraph* in order to teach the tabloids a lesson.

It was another quality paper, *The Times* no less, that Dorset listener Mrs Michael Johnson used when she started one of the greatest mass public-opinion campaigns of modern times: the SAVE NIGEL PARGETTER FROM AFRICA campaign – cruelly dubbed, by some, as the campaign to save Africa from Nigel. Victoria Johnson placed a small ad appealing for support – and support she got!

'Nigel and Nelson are inspired characters. Can it be true? Can he really be leaving? Nigel, poor Nigel, he does so want to be loved. Well we love him, don't we.'

Actors' union bl the death of Doris

By SIMON KINNERSLEY

DORIS ARCHER died last night—and the actors' union, Equity, blacked the hymn the BBC had recorded in a country church as background music.

Doris had to go because of the illness of Gwen Berryman, the actress who has played Dan for nearly 30 years.

Scriptwriter Bill Smethurst decided she should die while husband Dan was at evensong in the local church.

To create the right atmosphere, the BBC had recorded a hymn at a 13th century church near Stratford-upon-Avon.

But, Equity, the actors' union, decided yesterday th— professional singers have been used—block on th—

home, the Archers studios were in virtual chaos as the crucial programme was being re-edited.

Thankfully, Miss Berryman, 73-year-old of the problems at — quay nursing ho— is recove— strok—

can't let Doris go wi— psalm. But whe— from I've — plete

MAIL FLOODS IN AS 'DORIS ARCHER' MEETS TROUBLED EN

"DORIS Archer" awoke today to a massive postal delivery of bouquets of flowers, letters, and cards following her radio death.

Three million listeners heard — ght in an episode

Today actress Gwen Berryman, 75, who plays Doris, woke up in a Torquay nursing home to the aftermath of her tear-jerking end.

Still recovering from a stroke, Gwen was not taking calls personally.

Mrs. Betty Miller, owner of the Carrisbrooke Nursing Home, said: "There has been a substantial mail this morning, — letters, flowers and

Telephone messages have been coming in this morning asking how Gwen is.

"I expect she will be looking forward to opening all the cards and letters later today," said Mrs. Miller.

Gwen, who played Doris Archer for 30 years in the BBC tale of country folk, is said to be "quite well."

But, according to Mrs. Miller, on the advice of a consultant, the actress did not hear — end to spare her emotions. — really be living

through that traumatic minute on the radio, and we thought it unwise for her to listen."

Miss Berryman was written out of The Archers because she was too ill to continue.

Instead of listening, she watched television, and missed Doris fading out peacefully, found dead in her armchair.

The union dispute broke out when Equity told the BBC union members should have been used to sing a hymn and the Corporation, unable to comply in time, substituted a 20-

year-old rec— church congr— Meanwhile, into further funeral.

The BBC church cor— funeral and union me— been emplo—

"We'— negotiatio— today an— outcome — made," — man.

'I miss him dreadfully already and he's only been gone one day – and fancy sending him off without his parents there. How could you? You are definitely in my bad books.'

'Nigel, our gadfly gorilla, his character so sharply etched, should not be lost since it shows up those around him more clearly. If he must go, could he not at least go in real disgrace having seduced Jill?'

'Nigel should be saved by catching malaria on a weekend trip from Zimbabwe into Tanzania. He has to come home for tests. Everyone will worry about his health which could waver for a short while. On his return his Great Aunt Agatha could remember him in her will sufficiently dearly for him to buy Nelson's wine bar and be happy ever after.'

'Perhaps he will have a holiday in Zimbabwe and come back. I am sure he will be made welcome and have a smashing time. He need have no fear of the lions as there are very few left.' The 'Bring Back Nigel' campaign was a triumphant success, but then The Archers' listener has always been a force to reckon with!

Protest silences 'Archers' hymns

The actors' union Equity yesterday forced the BBC to scrap the original recording of last night's episode of "T Archers" in which Doris Arc dies

...ion claimed a recor ...ice which is ta found (

a London church yesterday. But they were unable to find an organist in time and used a record ...tead

The last act that 'Doris' missed

DORIS ARCHER — 75-year-old actress Gwen Berryman —awoke today to a massive delivery of flowers, letters, and cards following her radio "death."

Three million listeners heard her die in an episode rearranged because of objections by the actors' union Equity to the use of a genuine church congregation.

Gwen, recovering from a stroke, was not taking calls personally in a Torquay nursing home. She had played Doris for 30 years, and was written out of the series because of ill health.

On medical advice did not hear

Flowers for 'dead' Doris Archer

THE actress who plays Doris Archer awoke this morning to a massive postal delivery of bouquets, letters, and cards following her radio death.

Three million listeners heard her die last night in an episode hastily re-arranged at the last minute because of objections by the actors' union Equity to the use of a genuine church congregation.

This morning actress Gwen Berryman (75), who plays Doris, woke up in a Torquay nursing home to the aftermath of her tear-jerking end.

Still recovering from a stroke, Gwen was not taking calls personally

AMBRIDGE DILEMMA OVER DORIS

By DAVID JACK

PRODUCERS of BBC radio's "The Archers" are faced with a real-life dilemma over the future of one of the serial's best-loved characters.

Actress Gwen Berryman, who has played Doris Archer since the programme began in 1950, has suffered a stroke which has left her partially paralysed.

Programme chiefs have managed to keep her illness secret for almost nine months despite a series of changes in the storyline.

Because the programme is recorded weeks in advance, Doris Archer was last heard on air in April celebrating her 80th birthday.

Since then she has only been talked about on the programme—at first on holiday in the Channel Islands, and then when she was "too poorly to come downstairs."

Miss Berryman, who is 75, is still recovering from her stroke in a Torquay nursing home near her home.

Rigorous

Her speech has not been affected.

Programme chiefs are worried over whether she will recover sufficiently to cope with the six rigorous nine-and-a-half-hour rehearsal and recording sessions each month.

They have already ruled out the prospect of another actress taking over the role.

Now Mr Jock Gallag-

GWEN BERRYMAN
Suffered a stroke

her, Head of Radio at the BBC's "Pebble Mill" studios in Birmingham—home of "The Archers"—will be visiting Miss Berryman to assess her progress.

Mr Gallagher said yesterday: "Everyone is hoping she will be able to come back to us.

"Gwen has been very concerned that she is causing problems, but she would understand, whatever decision we finally have to make.

"Whatever decision is made, the BBC hopes Miss Berryman will be well enough to be in Birmingham programme

The Ambridge Story 1961-70

In 1961 Paul Johnson abandoned horse-owning and started taking lessons as a helicopter pilot. Here he demonstrates tractor hydraulics to a puzzled Ned Larkin and an admiring Jimmy Grange. Bill Payne (Ned), Leslie Dunn (Paul).

1961

Jimmy Grange, the singing farmhand, fell passionately in love with Carol Grey during guitar lessons and demanded that she break off her engagement to Charles Grenville. She refused.

Jennifer went on a school holiday to Switzerland and fell in love with a skiing instructor called Max. When he visited The Bull he turned out to be Max Bailey from Wolverhampton. Jack refused to let him stay the night.

Hazel, the five-year-old daughter of Valerie and Reggie Trentham, contracted polio.

Ambridge was hit by vandalism. Teenagers on motorbikes started a fire on the Grenville Estate and kicked Walter about the head until he was unconscious. Grenville arrived and broke one of the vandal's arms with a judo blow.

Tom and Pru fostered two boys, Peter Stevens and Johnny Martin.

Walter had a win on the pools and bought himself an eight-speed bicycle. Nelson reappeared in Ambridge.

Right: Jimmy Grange takes time off from his skiffle group to romance the lovely Hazel White, whose father, alas, was busy trying to blackmail Carol Tregorran. Mary Chester (Hazel White).

Below: Ned Larkin measures up the U-bend for a reason no longer apparent.

Carol married Charles Grenville, and was elected to the committee of Ambridge WI.

Ambridge Dairy Farmers was formed and Dan installed a bulk milk tank at Brookfield.

Phil returned to his old passion – cine photography. He and Jill made a 16mm colour film for the Ambridge Cine Club.

1962

John Tregorran's love letters to Carol were stolen from her bedroom by blackmailers who demanded £200 for their return. A trap was laid by PC Bryden, and the crooks caught – estate worker Harry White and his accomplice Chuck Ballard.

Aunt Laura tried to buy Brookfield for little Anthony William Daniel when he grew up. Dan told her to stop making trouble.

Jennifer entered a dairy queen contest at Borchester Young Farmers' Club and went abroad on holiday with Max.

Paul Johnson got a job as a helicopter pilot. He

While sister Jennifer went round with boys and entered beauty contests, Lilian Archer spent the summer doing odd jobs – trying to make five shillings a week to buy hay for her pony, Pensioner, in the winter. Margaret Lane (Lilian).

and Christine moved to Newmarket. Sally Johnson married racing ne'er do well Toby Stobeman and they opened a betting shop in Hollerton.

Phil started his specialist pig unit at Hollowtree.

Grenville took on a new farm manager – a 'good-looking Scotsman' called Andrew Sinclair.

Reggie and Valerie Trentham sold Grey Gables and left the village. The Country Club was bought by Birmingham businessman Jack Woolley. He announced that he was going to turn it into an exclusive holiday centre for tired businessmen.

Carol gave birth to a boy. He was named Richard Charles.

1963

John Tregorran fell in love with pretty, blue-eyed district nurse Janet Sheldon and married her in June.

Nelson announced that he now had a smart, sophisticated girlfriend whose parents were wealthy and influential. He sent Walter £10.

Young Brummie Sid Perks moved to the village and impressed Jack Woolley by exposing a rogue barman at Grey Gables. Jack gave Sid a job as chauffeur and general handyman. Woolley also opened a gift shop in Borchester and called it the 'New Curiosity Shop'.

Ambridge won the Borsetshire best-kept village competition. Jack and Peggy built a new dining room at The Bull.

Christine and Paul returned to Ambridge, and rented Wynford's farmhouse from Phil.

Jennifer started a teacher training course in Walsall.

Janet Tregorran was killed in a car crash and Charles Grenville was badly injured. Surgeons at Borchester General Hospital amputated one of his legs.

A champagne dinner for Carol and husband Oliver Charles Grenville. In the autumn he was involved in a terrible car crash and lost one of his legs. Michael Shaw (Grenville).

Dan's shepherd, Len Thomas, failed to get a good job in Wales and started beating his wife and rabble-rousing among the Ambridge farm labourers.

Nelson and his sophisticated girlfriend were horrified to find Walter working as Father Christmas in a Borchester store.

1964

Dan and Doris took a foreign holiday for the first time – a fortnight in Malaga with Fred Barratt.

Reggie Trentham died in the West Indies. Valerie returned home with her little daughter Hazel. Jack Woolley went on a cruise and asked her to look after Grey Gables for him.

Newcomers to Ambridge included farmworker Gregory Salt and PC Albert Bates, who replaced PC Bryden as the village bobby.

Walter Gabriel opened a maggot-breeding business then bought a hot-air balloon from a Mr Snout of Hollerton.

Sid Perks was attacked by louts at Hollerton Fair. They stole his motorbike and embarrassed his new girlfriend, Polly Mead.

Village schoolmistress Elsie Catcher told Jill that Shula was a backward child.

Charles Grenville was fitted with an artificial leg. In the Autumn he sold many of his business interests and went to America.

Walter Gabriel bought a stuffed gorilla and called it George. At Christmas he played Long John Silver in the vicar's production of *Treasure Island*. He had a real parrot.

Dan gave Doris a Jack Russell terrier for Christmas. They called it Trigger.

Walter Gabriel was in his prime – one minute breeding maggots, the next buying stuffed gorillas, hot-air balloons, and a steam engine he called 'Gabrielle'.

1965

Charles Grenville collapsed and died in America. Part of the estate was bought by Jack Woolley, and part by newcomer Ralph Bellamy.

Doris bought a pony and trap. In May she represented Ambridge WI at a Buckingham Palace Garden Party.

Gregory Salt proposed to Polly Mead, the barmaid at The Bull, but she turned him down. Sid Perks proposed and she accepted.

Walter Gabriel gave his parrot from *Treasure Island* to Mrs Twelvetrees of Felpersham then bought an elephant called Rosie. Before long she had a baby called Tiny Tim.

Above: Peggy looks pensively at The Bull. In the summer she and Jack opened a new dining room, and Aunt Laura gave them £30,000 to pay for it. Jack bought Jennifer a moped so that she could return home more often.

Right: Gamekeeper Tom Forrest gives Jack Woolley a few hints about shooting. In the spring Woolley bought half of Grenville's estate, and in the autumn he bought a large topaz brooch for Valerie Trentham and asked her to marry him. Bob Arnold (Tom), Philip Garston-Jones (Woolley).

Opposite: Dan and Doris look out from the Brookfield rose trellis. In the summer they went on holiday to Ireland. While they were there Brookfield was burgled and Doris's famous collection of copperware was stolen.

The Ambridge Summer Festival was organised by John Tregorran. It included a pageant depicting the Garden of Eden. Rosie and Tiny Tim were a huge success.

Aunt Laura hired 'handsome, dark-haired' Roger Patillo as a chauffeur. In November he confessed that he was not a suspicious foreigner (as Jack thought), but was Roger Travers-Macy, going round in disguise because his family were cold and indifferent to him.

Jennifer was thrown out of her flat in Walsall after a rowdy student party.

Jack Woolley and Valerie Trentham became engaged.

Christine and Paul adopted a little boy called Peter.

1966

Ambridge was hit by a wave of arson. Brookfield was set alight, then several other farms and hayricks. The arsonist – caught setting fire to The Bull – was revealed as Polly Mead's father.

Walter Gabriel found 42 gold sovereigns hidden up the chimney of Honeysuckle Cottage. Nelson went into partnership with Toby Stobeman and they opened the Borchester Casino.

Woolley married Valerie Trentham and Sid married Polly Mead (Jennifer and Lilian were bridesmaids). Woolley took on a new chauffeur and general handyman called Higgs.

John Tregorran opened a bookshop in Borchester

Dan leans on a stick after slipping a disc, and watches Doris tend the Brookfield garden.

and took on Roger Travers-Macy as his assistant. The dairy manager at Brookfield, Paddy Redmond, brought his girlfriend over from Ireland. She was called Nora McAuley and she worked as a barmaid at The Bull.

Jack Woolley turned Arkwright Hall into a recreation centre, with a swimming pool that converted into a dance hall in winter. He gave Sid the job of manager.

Jack Archer started gambling heavily at Nelson's casino. After a big win he gave Peggy a gold wrist watch, but she later found he had paid £450 in gaming debts. Peggy was even more horrified to discover that Jennifer was secretly going out with the suddenly prosperous Nelson.

John Tregorran proposed to Carol, and was accepted.

Jill became pregnant and so did Jennifer.

Walter and Nelson disappeared. Road-mender Zebedee Tring claimed he saw them heading for Southampton.

1967

Jennifer announced that she was pregnant but refused to name the father.

Walter Gabriel returned to Ambridge after a fabulous cruise. Nelson was reported killed after a light plane crashed in the English Channel. Villagers bought Walter a tank of goldfish to cheer him up.

John Tregorran married Carol. He sold the bookshop and they bought Manor Court, Ambridge, for £20,000.

Paddy Redmond quarrelled with Phil about a milk bonus scheme, abused his girlfriend Nora McAuley, and left Ambridge. He was later exposed as the father of Jennifer's baby.

Sid Perks was sacked fom Arkwright Hall and went to work for Phil at Hollowtree pig unit. Disliking pigs he then moved on to work for a mysterious Mr Brown

at Paunton's Farm. Mistrusting Mr Brown he went to work for Paul Johnson at the village garage.

Jennifer gave birth to a baby boy and called him Adam. Jill gave birth to a daughter, Elizabeth, who immediately underwent a hole-in-the-heart operation.

Police raided Paunton's Farm after a mailvan robbery and found Nelson's fingerprints on a whiskey glass. Then French police claimed that Nelson was still alive and involved in shady Continental activities. Village girl Nancy Tarrant from Penny Hassett claimed that Nelson had made her pregnant.

Burglars ransacked Brookfield and knocked Doris unconscious.

Left: Sixties girl Jennifer Archer, expecting a baby by Phil's cowman Paddy Redmond. Angela Piper (Jennifer).

Below: Lambing time for Ned Larkin, 1967.

1968

Nelson Gabriel was tracked down by Interpol and brought back to England. He was charged with armed robbery but acquitted at Gloucester Assizes. Walter said that Nelson had been 'framed'.

Doris recovered from her attack by burglars and received £250 from the Criminal Injuries Compensation Board.

Phil went on a round-the-world farming tour. When he returned he said it was time for Dan to retire.

Paul Johnson opened a coffee bar at the village garage and claimed it would soon become the 'in place' to be. It didn't. His bank told him he was going bankrupt.

Jack Archer won £245 at the Borchester Casino and drank himself senseless. Peggy begged him to develop new interests, so he and Walter Gabriel bought a boat and kept it on the Severn.

Lilian had an affair with Roger Travers-Macy then

Snowy has kittens, and Peggy is cheered-up. She was having a hard time because of Jack's gambling and drinking habits. June Spencer (Peggy).

fell in love with Canadian Air Force pilot Lester Nicholson. Jennifer had an affair with Roger Travers-Macy then married him.

There were two new arrivals in Ambridge – Hugo Barnaby, a cousin of John Tregorran, and David Latimer the new vicar.

The Reverend David Latimer took over as vicar of Ambridge. Churchwarden Tom Forrest was upset by the new vicar's 'easygoing ways' and refused to call him by his Christian name.

Polly Perks won £1,000 on a premium bond and used it as a deposit to buy the village shop.

Dan was presented with an illuminated address by the NFU to mark forty years' faithful and active service to agriculture.

1969

Dan was seriously ill in hospital with a chest infection. He agreed to go into semi-retirement.

Paul Johnson sold the garage to Ralph Bellamy and set up a small engineering firm in Borchester.

Jill was elected to the Rural District Council.

Polly Perks became pregnant, but lost the baby when thugs raided the village shop and attacked her and Walter Gabriel.

Jack Archer lost interest in his boat and started drinking again. He insisted on opening a 'Playbar' at The Bull with fruit machines and expresso coffee.

Tony Archer bought himself a scooter and started going out with the vicar's daughter, Tessa Latimer.

Jack Woolley (*left*) views his broad acres with fellow 'squire' Ralph Bellamy. Bellamy, however, was not pleased. He had his eyes on lovely Lilian Bellamy, but she was determined to marry a Canadian. Jack Holloway (Ralph Bellamy).

Above: Carol Tregorran calls round for tea at Brookfield, and confides to Doris that she is expecting a baby.

Sid Perks at The Bull. In the summer he was busy helping to re-form the Ambridge cricket team. Alan Devereux (Sid).

When Tessa was unkind to him he threatened to emigrate.

Carol Tregorran gave birth to a baby girl, Anna Louise.

Walter Gabriel opened a short-stay caravan site next to Honeysuckle Cottage and called it 'The Old Mill Piece'.

Youths ran amok in the 'Playbar' at The Bull and smashed up the tables and chairs.

1970

Jennifer's son Adam was kidnapped from outside The Bull. Police at first suspected Sid Perks. The kidnappers were tracked down in Birmingham, and Adam rescued.

Dan and Doris moved into Glebe Cottage. Phil, Jill, and the family moved into Brookfield. Jack complained about the farm going to his younger brother.

Ambridge baker Doughy Hood shows his talent for putting ships into bottles. Arnold Ridley (Doughy Hood).

Tony sent for details about emigrating to Australia. He changed his mind when Bellamy made him Dairy Manager on his estate.

Walter Gabriel found £500 stuffed down the back of an old armchair. Police suspected it was part of the Great Mailvan Robbery haul. Nelson said he had hidden the money in the chair as 'a surprise for my father.'

Lilian and Lester Nicholson went to Canada, where Lester died in hospital. Lilian returned to Ambridge.

Fire gutted part of Manor Court, Carol and John Tregorran moved in with Jack Woolley at Grey Gables.

Arthur Perkins died in London and Mrs P returned to Ambridge. Walter proposed to her (without success) and gave her a budgerigar.

Nelson Gabriel was revealed as the mystery owner of Hollowtree Flats – a new, luxurious development in the old Hollowtree Farmhouse. He asked Lilian to look after them for him.

Jennifer gave birth to a baby girl, Deborah.

5

Christmas at Ambridge

Some Christmases from long ago

Christmas Eve 1952 and both Christine and Grace were in a state of high excitement as they mucked out the stables. 'I say,' gasped Christine, 'we ought to give the stable boy a Christmas box, oughtn't we?' and Grace said, 'Gosh, yes! I'm glad you reminded me!' and they agreed to put a pound in his pay packet with a little note. Elsewhere in the village young madcap Philip was giving Tom Forrest a lift in his motor-car. 'I'm just takin' a few rabbits and such round the village from Squire,' Tom said, 'to 'elp out wi' the Christmas table,' and young Philip replied heartily, 'Good Old Squire!' and Tom reminisced about the days when the Squire's old mother used to 'go out regular every Christmas Eve in 'er carriage and pair, all loaded up wi' vittles and suchlike.' Despite the festive season Philip was depressed because nobody wanted to buy his motor-car, and Tom said, helpfully, 'I 'ave heard tell the bottom's dropped out o' the used-car market,' and added: ''Tis Christmas, y'know, and folks is more interested now in fillin' their bellies than fillin' their garridges.'

At Mrs Perkin's cottage, Jack Archer was being ordered to spend Christmas Eve looking after little Lilian and little Jennifer and baby Anthony. Jack was very sulky. He wanted to spend Christmas Eve in The Bull and didn't see why he should change his plan just because his wife Peggy was in hospital with diphtheria.

Lunch at Brookfield was shepherd's pie, and on hearing that Dan and Christine had already started theirs, Philip cried out: 'Golly! Come on! If we don't get a move on the blighters won't leave any for us!' After lunch Dan sought out Simon Cooper, the loyal Brookfield farmhand, who was busy splitting logs in the yard. Dan told him he could have Christmas Day off from milking, then said: 'You come here a minute, you old faggot!' A puzzled Simon said, 'Why, what's up then, gaffer? Sommat wrong?' and Dan said: 'Here stick this envelope in your pocket. Call it a Christmas Box if you want to. . '

'Oh, thank ye kindly, gaffer. . . '

'But what I'm calling it is a share in the profits on the chrysanths.'

Christmas Eve in the Brookfield parlour found everyone busy wrapping presents. Dan disguised his traditional £5 gift to Doris by putting it in a shoebox, and Doris became very emotional and exclaimed: 'A box! Oh Dan – don't tell me you've actually bought me a present for once instead of just giving me the money!' and Philip hooted and chortled with glee. Christine, though, was in sombre mood, sobbing over Valerie Grayson (later to be Valerie Woolley, mother of the appalling Hazel) who had come to the village recently and did not have any friends. 'She's only got Reggie … I've … I've got my whole family. I'm luckier than she is and – well – I – I can afford to be kind.' The evening ended with two stray boy carol singers from Hollerton being asked into their parlour to sing with the family and eat mince pies.

Events in Ambridge were not heard on Christmas Day 1952, but at the Boxing Day shoot Tom Forrest was discovered grovelling to the Squire's nephew, smoothie Clive Lawson-Hope. 'Not quite enough

Opposite: Christmas Day, 1959, and Dan smiles happily as he prepares to carve the turkey.

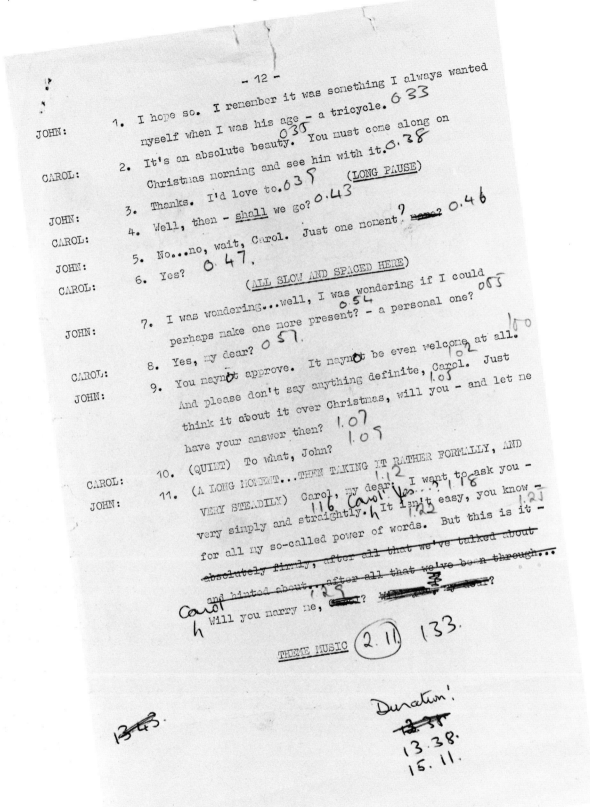

- 12 -

JOHN: 1. I hope so. I remember it was something I always wanted myself when I was his age - a tricycle. 6.33 0.35

CAROL: 2. It's an absolute beauty. You must come along on Christmas morning and see him with it. 0.38

JOHN: 3. Thanks. I'd love to. 0.39 (LONG PAUSE)
4. Well, then - shall we go? 0.43

CAROL: 5. No...no, wait, Carol. Just one moment? none? 0.46

JOHN: 6. Yes? 0.47.

(ALL SLOW AND SPACED HERE)

CAROL: 7. I was wondering...well, I was wondering if I could 0.55 0.54 perhaps make one more present? - a personal one?

JOHN: 8. Yes, my dear? 0.57

CAROL: 9. You maynot approve. It maynot be even welcome at all. 1.00 1.02 And please don't say anything definite, Carol. Just

JOHN: think it about it over Christmas, will you - and let me 1.05 have your answer then? 1.07 1.09

CAROL: 10. (QUIET) To what, John?

JOHN: 11. (A LONG MOMENT...THEN TAKING IT RATHER FORMALLY, AND VERY STEADILY) Carol, my dear: I want to ask you - 1.12 1.18 very simply and straightly. Carol, Yes...? It isn't easy, you know - 116 1.23 for all my so-called power of words. But this is it - 1.25 absolutely firmly, after all that we've talked about and hinted about, after all that we've been through... Carol Will you marry me, ⟨⟨⟨⟨⟩⟩⟩? ⟨⟨⟨⟩⟩? 1.25

THEME MUSIC (2.11) 133.

13.43.

Duration:
2.55.
13.38.
15.11.

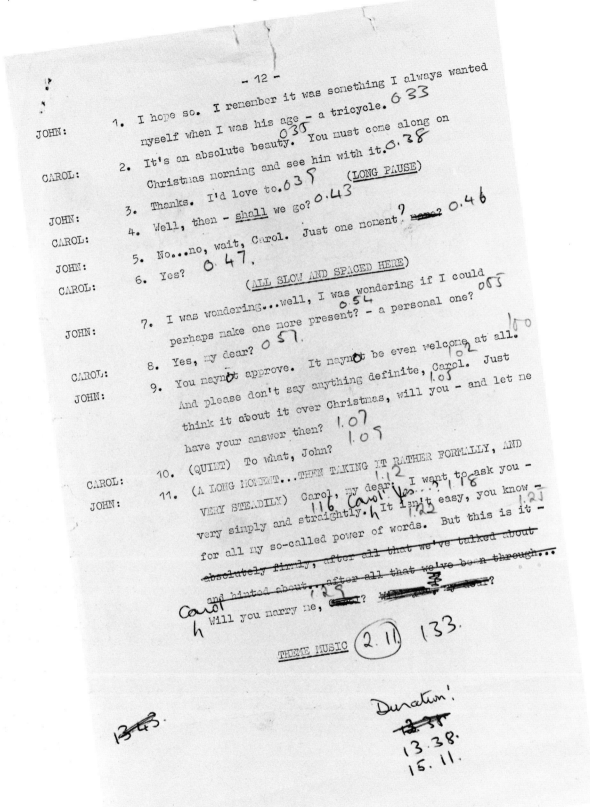

Christmas 1966 ... and John Tregorran proposes to Carol.

beaters I'm afraid, Mr Clive,' said Tom. 'Wi' your uncle takin' some of 'em for earth stoppin' I couldn't get enough.' Mr Clive generously forgave him.

Later, back in the village, Walter Gabriel recounted how he had helped little Jennifer to dress her dolls on Christmas Day, and Tom chipped in heartily: 'What do you know about petticoats, you old faggot?' to which Walter replied, 'You'd be surprised, me boy, you'd be surprised,' and confessed that he had an old flannel petticoat of his grannie's and used it as a bedspread. 'Bedspread?' exclaimed Tom, heartier than ever, 'I bet he wears it as a nightie!'

A year later it was the Home Service announcer who set the scene for Christmas Day in Ambridge. 'Early this morning as the smoke began to climb lazily out of the chimneys the village had a Sunday morning look,' he reported. 'No early bus, no clinking of milk bottles, no surge of children's voices as the time for the schoolbell draws near ... ' At Brookfield Farm, Len Thomas and Dan were heard being busy with milking. 'There were high jinks at The Bull last night,' said Len, and described how Walter had worn one of Peggy's best hats to do the can-can in the public bar.

After breakfast presents were opened in the parlour. Chris and Philip had bought Doris a nice warm dressing gown, and she assured them she would wear it only for 'high days and holidays.' Roguish Philip had bought his sister some nylon knickers and a slip, which prompted the puzzled comment from Dan: 'Blest if I know about you young Phil ... fancy giving your sister an underset.'

Christine gave Philip a fancy waistcoat ('the very same pattern I've been admiring in Faradays!') and he also got a cigarette case engraved with: 'To Phil ... with love from Grace, Christmas 1953.'

Later Christine gave Philip a sisterly warning about Anne Trentham, whom he was to partner to a dance the following night. 'She's very luscious, isn't she?' probed Christine, and Philip said, 'Jolly nice girl,' and Christine said, 'You mind and behave yourself, young Phil,' and Philip said, 'Don't worry, you know me,' and Christine said, 'That's the trouble ... I do know you.'

In the house Walter was getting very merry. 'This bitter tastes of necktie!' he announced, and Dan said, 'Of all the nerve!' and Walter chortled, 'Necktie of the Gods!'

Then came Christmas Lunch, with all the family round the kitchen table, even baby Tony (too young even to call for a can of lager) in his high chair. 'Oh crackers, I do love crackers,' lisped little Jennifer, and Jack was very jovial and kissed his mother-in-law, Mrs Perkins, and she said: 'My Golly, Master Jack!' and Christine said, 'Merry Christmas Jack, you old sinner!'

Dan carved the turkey ('Tender as Mrs P's heart and done to a turn') and after they had eaten he made the first of his famous (not to say regal) Christmas toasts. 'This kitchen of ours ain't by any means small,' he said, 'but it's not big enough – nor a hundred like it – to hold all our friends ... all the folk who've been good enough to let us know as they like us. I wish they could all be with us – or us with them – it'd be a wonderful party! But whoever they are, and wherever they are, in town or countryside, at home or in hospital ... here's to them all. We're proud and pleased to call them our friends. God bless 'em ... and a very merry Christmas to each and every one of them!'

'To all our absent friends,' chimed in Mrs P, and Walter, and Doris, and Phil and Chris, and Jack and Peggy, and the children (except for baby Anthony), 'God Bless you and a merry Christmas.' Then they went into the parlour to play housey-housey.

Two years went by. In the world at large food rationing ended. Roger Bannister ran a mile in under four minutes, and the Conservatives were returned to power. Independent television began, and in Ambridge Grace Archer (who had married Phil in April 1955) was killed in a stables fire. Christmas at Brookfield was a sad, reflective occasion. On Christmas Day, after tea, most of the family gathered in the parlour where Tom sang a song about turnips, and Dan and Doris warbled through their old favourite, 'Down the Vale'.

The happiest member of the family was Christine, who was spending the festive season at the home of dashing horse-owner Paul Johnson. On Christmas night they walked in the garden, and Paul said, 'Well, young Chris ... enjoying yourself?' and Christine replied, 'Immensely, thanks. Your people have been absolutely charming.'

'No inferiority complex?' inquired Paul, rather oddly, and when Christine assured him that she wasn't feeling at all inferior he murmured, 'You look very lovely by moonlight.'

Christ
i

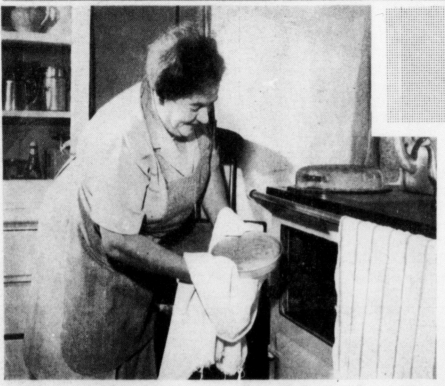

The turkey is trussed ready for the oven, bacon and eggs are sizzling on the stove, but there is still that sponge cake to make. A sponge, laced with fresh cream, is a regular Christmas Day treat at Brookfield Farm.

Under their leader, Tom Forre
forty minutes before the ser

But not everyone is surrounde
widowed Mrs. Turvey is typica
Christmas Day as at other time
her Christmas dinner—the bird

And now it's dinner time

Dan sharpens the carving knife in readiness for the long-awaited Christmas dinner. Christine, who has dropped in, feels that Pru's table decoration needs one or two last-minute adjustments.

as *Ambridge*

After church—out into the nippy morning air. There's Tom, Peggy, Dan, Doris, Grenville, Philip, Walter, Mrs. Turvey and Christine. But who's that talking to Philip? We'll let you into a secret — it's Ned's sister-in-law, Clarice.

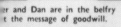
r and Dan are in the belfry
t the message of goodwill.

nd family at Christmas. The usands who are as lonely on With whom shall she share the bird-table in her garden?

Someone has to work on Christmas Day. In the thin sunshine of late afternoon, Jimmy Grange brings in the cows for milking, watched by Chris, Phil and Peggy from the yard of Brookfield Farm.

'Thank you, Mr Johnson,' said Christine ('shakily' according to the script) and a moment later Paul suddenly said, 'Heck! I knew there was something very important I hadn't done!' and kissed her. 'Hey ... *Hey!!!* gasped Christine, so worried was she that they might be seen.

Five Christmases later, married and living in Ambridge, they were no longer, alas, seeking private little walks in the moonlight. On Christmas Eve 1960 Paul first confessed to having received a cigarette lighter ('Gas job, too, worth over five quid') from a girl called Marianne Peters, then tried to wriggle off to his office Christmas party. 'Don't celebrate too much before you get home,' snapped a carping Chris, 'remember we've still a lot of Christmas preparations to finish. I'll expect you at what time?'

'Ooooh ... difficult ... you know how it is,' said Paul, reasonably, and Christine said, acidly: 'Not later than seven ... and wipe all the lipstick off before you get home.'

It was a worldly and depressing Christmas for almost everyone. Charles Grenville had opened a packing factory in Ambridge and was horribly gruff when he discovered his workers slipping seasonal tots of whiskey into their tea. 'I've a feeling the daily output figures will be down,' he complained, and John Tregorran told him he had more than whiskey to worry about. A gang of thugs from Hollerton was loitering about the village behaving in a menacing manner. 'They might get a perverted kick out of sabotaging your factory,' said John, and Grenville declared his intention of writing an article for the *Borchester Echo* demanding the return of corporal punishment. John was horrified. 'When the teddy-boy toughs see that,' he warned, 'they'll have another rod in pickle for you.'

Even at Brookfield, Christmas started off with depressing overtones. Dan wondered why so many cards were religious, and Doris said it was because so many folk were frightened of the H bomb.

On Christmas Eve, though, things cheered up when the Forrests' foster children, Peter and Johnny, came into the parlour and sang 'Once in Royal David's City', and at the end of the episode it was Peter's piping voice that said, 'A jolly Merry Christmas Uncle Tom ... and you Auntie Pru,' and Johnny who said, 'And to everybody everywhere ... the best Christmas ever!'

The Ambridge Christmas Concert (an institution that was to out-last the Brookfield Christmas Toast) was introduced in 1962 and John Tregorran had everyone in fits when he introduced Walter and Ned as 'Cliff Pilchard and Elvis Measley'. It was a quiet Christmas Eve at Brookfield. Chris and Paul had moved to Newmarket, and Phil and Jill were living at Coombe Farm, and Dan and Doris sat alone by the flickering apple-log fire. 'Another Christmas, and we're still sitting by our own bright fireside,' remarked Doris, setting the scene. 'And we're still having a crowd of friends and relatives to help us enjoy the great day,' said Dan, firmly, reaching for the sherry bottle and proposing a toast. 'Here's to us and to our family,' he said, and Doris called out, 'A happy Christmas, everybody!' even though Dan was the only other person in the room.

On Christmas afternoon there was a party in the parlour and everyone sang 'Bless This House' and 'Ten Green Bottles', a rather predictable offering that was greatly improved in 1963 when the Brookfield Christmas party was convulsed by Ned and Walter singing 'Old Ambridge in the Vale':

> At *old* Ambridge in the Vale,
> Our Christmas only comes up once a ye-ar.
> At *old* Ambridge in the Vale,
> We celebrate wi' Walter's nettle be-er.
> But when the Boss an' Missus
> Has had more than one or two —
> *They* celebrate wi' kisses,
> Jest to prove that love is true.
> And all of us a-lookin' on says 'Hey, Boss, after you!'
> At *old* Ambridge in the Vale [two-three-four]
> [EVERYONE JOINS IN WITH LAUGHTER]
> O-o-old Ambridge in the Vale! ...
> [CROSS-FADE WITH THEME MUSIC]

Walter Gabriel was still in fine fettle three years later in 1966 when he came bouncing into the Brookfield parlour on Christmas day with a cry of, 'Here's ole gallant knight Sir Walter a-goin' down on his poor ole knees an' presenting his bee-youtious hostess wi' a nice Christmas posy.' The script then instructed

Opposite: Elizabeth Archer and Brian Aldridge star in the Ambridge Christmas Revue – 'A glittering galaxy of breathtaking talent' (*Borchester Echo*). Alison Dowling (Elizabeth), Charles Collingwood (Brian).

GENERAL CLAPS AND RESPOND followed by wicked Walter saying to Doris, 'You'm like the Queen Mary herself bein' launched – all we needs is a bottle o' the ole bubbly to brek on that boosy o' yours!'

'Cept it'd bounce straight off again!' chortled Dan, 'right back in your eye, Walter lad!'

'Now none of it!' cried Doris. 'The very idea . . . I know this dress is a bit daring for me . . . '

Later Walter lapsed, curiously, into Irish, when he said, 'D'y'know what I'm a-going to do? I'm a-going to ask this be-yew-ti-ful hostess o' ours to propose a toast, so I am!' What followed was perhaps the last of the great Brookfield Christmas toasts . . .

'Good friends – and all other good friends, wherever you are, all over the world . . . I give you all every best wish for Christmas. May you all have a happy holiday over this sacred season . . . God Bless you all.'

A seasonal joke at Brookfield Farm, Christmas Day, 1985. Timothy Bentinck (David), Patricia Greene (Jill), Alison Dowling (Elizabeth), Moir Leslie (Sophie).

The Archers Christmas Quiz

1 What did Walter Gabriel try to make for Mrs P in Coronation Year?

2 Who was Phil's rival in the courting of Grace Fairbrother?

3 Who did Tom Forrest accidentally shoot in the woods in 1957?

4 Where did Phil propose to Jill?

5 What did Lettie Lawson-Hope leave to Doris in her will?

6 Where did Reggie Trentham die?

7 What unusual pet did Walter buy in 1965?

8 What was Roger Travers-Macy's pseudonym?

9 Who was Nelson's partner in the Borchester Casino?

10 Who is Adam Macy's real father?

11 What was Nora Salt's maiden name?

12 What instrument does George Barford play?

13 Where has Alf Grundy been for several years?

14 What was the last unsuccessful business venture of Paul Johnson's?

15 Name the Alridges' German au-pair in the early eighties.

16 Name Terry Barford's regiment.

17 Who was Eddie Grundy's first fiancée?

18 Who fell in love with Jennifer in 1980?

19 Who made love to Shula in a stubblefield?

20 Who did Shula set off round the world with?

21 Who were Shula's bridesmaids?

22 Who forced his attentions on Lilian in Hollowtree Flats?

23 Who lives in
a) Keeper's Cottage?
b) Woodbine Cottage?
c) Willow Farm?
d) Lower Loxley House?
e) Number 6, The Green?
f) Rose Cottage?

24 What was the name of
a) Jethro's wife?
b) Martha's husband?
c) Joe's wife?
d) Joe's father?
e) Jack Woolley's wife?

25 Who owns the following dogs
a) Gyp?
b) Georgina?
c) Bessie?

26 What tunes did Nigel's ice-cream van play in 1985?

27 Where was Nelson found after he ran off after Hebe?

28 What did Martin the Vet give Walter to cheer him up?

29 What did D. S. Barry lend Eddie when Grange Farm was burgled?

30 What name did Wayne and Jolene give to their baby?

31 Who first lodged with Mrs Antrobus at Nightingale Farm?

32 Who was secretary of Ambridge WI in 1986?

33 Who edits the parish magazine?

34 Who organises the local meals-on-wheels?

35 Who was local agricultural union secretary after Mike Tucker?

36 What did Aunt Laura run?

37 Why did Nigel get the sack from Underwoods?

38 Who were Mark and Shula's first official guests at the Woolmarket flat?

39 What useful gift did Jennifer give Dan for his eighty-ninth birthday?

40 Who directed the Grey Gables promo video?

41 What bible story caused Joe to quarrel with the vicar?

42 Who died while looking after the cattle at Bridge Farm?

43 What dramatic change of appearance did Phil undergo in 1985?

44 Who was blamed for the death of Eddie's favourite ferret, Tex?

45 Where did Sid go to convalesce after his ulcer operation?

46 What trick did Captain fail to perform at the village fête?

47 Who prepared the food at Nelson's before Shane?

48 What gifts did Nigel bring back from Africa?

49 Who sang at Elizabeth's party in the barn?

50 What did Jack Woolley advertise in the *Guardian*?

Answers on page 64

AN AMBRIDGE

GHOST STORY

The Terrible Tale of Chicken Charlie and the Great Christmas Darts Match of 1932

[*As told by Joseph Grundy*]

I suppose the most famous ghost in these parts is the Wandering White Lady of Loxley Barratt, who pops up now and again moaning and crying for her drowned lover. And the most fearsome I suppose is the Hob Hound of Edgeley, with his burning red eyes and his poisonous breath, who runs the Hassett Hills on stormy winter's nights with a wild huntsman chasing along behind him.

But for my money the most pitiful, heartbreaking ghost is that of Chicken Charlie, who appears in St Stephen's churchyard, here in Ambridge, on December the twenty-second each year and throws imaginary darts at the church clock.

Now I don't know if any of you can remember Chicken Charlie, but he was a mean, runtish sort of bloke who used to go round with Foxy Sugden and Snatch Foster's dad in the days when The Cat and Fiddle was a drinking man's pub and nobody had heard of lemonade shandies and toasted pâté sandwiches.

Oh, it was a rough place all right, with stinking sawdust on the floors, and lamps that didn't get their wicks trimmed in a month of Sundays, and home-brewed beer as thick as porridge, and a landlord called Webster who used to go to Dartmoor for his holidays. The only respectable soul in the pub was the barmaid, Rosie, and she was a charity girl from Borchester Orphanage who saved her sixpences, week after week, hoping to make enough to escape from that den of vice and iniquity. It never happened, mind. She married Webster in the end and they had ten children.

Anyway, to get back to Chicken Charlie. It was December the nineteenth, 1932, and it was the night of the annual darts match between The Bull and The Cat and Fiddle, and my Dad took me along, nipper though I was, and sat me in a corner of the bar, and Rosie, bless her, gave me a mug of skimmed milk and a Worcester apple, and that night I watched the best darts match there's been in South Borset this century.

Never, in all history, have two teams been so evenly matched! The Bull had Tom Forrest's old man and John Gabriel, and Silas Winter of course – he was in his prime was Silas in those days. And as for The Cat and Fiddle, well, with Alf Blower and Snatch Foster's dad and young Foxy Sugden, not to mention Chicken Charlie, you can see they was a team in a million.

The match started about seven o'clock, when a shoebox was placed on the bartop, a slit was cut in its lid, and each member of each team put a bob in.

That was just for starters. After that, whenever a player scored one-eighty or a bull the opposition team had to cough up another tanner each, and the same when each game was won. It was one of those harmless old customs guaranteed to end up in a few heads being split open one way or another.

Chicken Charlie, ice-cool when he aimed his arrows but trembling like a leaf when he downed his cider, and he had reason to tremble, poor devil, because they were chucking him out of his poultry farm on New Year's Day if he didn't find twenty pounds rent, and there he was, within an ace of winning the jackpot!

There were thirteen sets, and by 8.30 twelve of them had been played, six to The Cat and Fiddle and six to The Bull, and after a break for Rosie to bring round black pudding and pickled-onion sandwiches – and another Worcester apple for me, bless her sweet young heart – the teams settled down for the last set.

I can picture that scene as if it were yesterday. The grey, grimy walls. The smoke from the lamps round the darts board. The stench of stale beer, and sweating humanity ... it was a real pub, not the sort of French boudoir they've turned them into nowadays!

And there was Silas Winter in his moleskin breeches – him being a keeper of course – and

It was the last, deciding game of the evening. Chicken Charlie had scored two one-eighties, then a treble nineteen and a treble eighteen. He raised his arm, his hand was poised, nobody dared hardly breathe as he tensed for the shot – a double fifteen, that was all it needed – and at that moment the door opened and the vicar of Ambridge came in followed by a dozen little choirboys singing 'God Rest Ye Merry Gentlemen.'

I've heard of some brave men in my time. Captain Oates, in the Antarctic. That young lad who stood on the burning deck. Admiral Lord Nelson. But when that vicar with his shining scrubbed face beamed round and held up his collection box and asked for a penny for the Borchester Orphan's Christmas Dinner, well he was the bravest or stupidest man that I've ever known. And when he said perhaps the assembled company would like to join him and his little choristers in a seasonal song or two – well, I thought he'd be flying out of the window head first into the horse trough before he could blink.

It didn't happen though.

No, and this says a lot about human nature. They reckon there's some bad in the best of us – and a little bit of good in the worst.

It's true. I know it, because Foxy Sugden, and Snatch Foster's dad, and Chicken Charlie, stood up in the bar of The Cat and Fiddle on the night of December the nineteenth, 1932, and they sung 'Once in Royal David's City' and 'Away in a Manger', and Rosie the barmaid went round with the Vicar's collection box while grown men dug deep into their pockets, and then she gave it back to the vicar, and he shook the box about and said 'God bless you all,' with tears in his eyes, and off into the night he went with his little choirboys trilling 'Wassail, wassail, all over the town.'

Thirty seconds later, and Chicken Charlie scored his double fifteen, and The Cat and Fiddle mob yelled with joy, and everybody shouted 'How much has he won then?' and Webster the landlord opened the box on the bartop and said, 'One and sixpence halfpenny and two trouser buttons.'

You've realised what happened, of course. While the choir's box was circulating around it somehow got mixed up with The Cat and Fiddle box – it was that dark and smokey you couldn't tell one from the other – and that accounted for the vicar being so thankful to everybody!

Well, Chicken Charlie leapt for the door like a tiger, half a dozen of his mates behind him, and if they'd caught them choirboys they'd have been singing soprano for the rest of their lives, but fortunately for them the Hollerton omnibus was passing at the time, and Chicken Charlie went right under it,

and in all the excitement the vicar and his choirboys got clean away.

A sad story. He was dead, of course, dead as one of his own chickens. And they buried him three days later.

Now I daresay you think that's the end of my tale, and there's probably a couple of unanswered questions in your mind. First of all, you're probably wondering how those two collection boxes got muddled up, and although I can't say for certain, I can tell you that I caught, in the lamplight, a glimpse of Rosie's face when the discovery was made, and it had what I can only call a look of triumph and satisfaction on it, and as I told you earlier, she did come from Borchester Orphanage herself . . .

And the other question, of course, is 'What's Chicken Charlie's ghost doing haunting St Stephen's churchyard if he was killed outside The Cat and Fiddle?'

Well, you know, it takes a great deal to make a poor spirit come back and wander this world. Anguish, and heartache, like the Wandering White Lady of Loxley Barratt; or blind, horrible terror like the Hob Hound of Edgeley with its red, burning eyes and its poisonous breath. Chicken Charlie had lost twenty quid and fallen under a bus, and that's all a poor tenant farmer can expect in this world, when all's said and done. I daresay I'll go that way myself if the Farmer's Lung don't get me first.

No, the writhing torment came three days later when they buried him, and that vicar and his choirboys came and gathered round his grave, and the vicar said what a generous man he was, and how much he'd done for the Borchester orphans, and then the choirboys sang 'Mine Eyes Hath Seen the Glory' when all they'd really seen was a pile of Chicken Charlie's shillings and tanners and ten bob notes . . .

Turn in his grave? He spun faster than a power drill and he's spinning there yet, out there in the churchyard, aiming his feeble, ghostly fingers at the church clock, and trying, on the stroke of midnight, for another double fifteen.

'The Village Pump'

[As sung by Mr Tom Forrest at the Ambridge Christmas Revue]

There's a pretty little village far away,
Where they grows new potatoes, corn and hay,
There's a tricklin' little rill,
That works a little mill,
And the mill it keeps a-workin' all the day.
There's a lot of little 'ouses in the middle,
And two pubs, The Bull and Cat and Fiddle,
But you make no mistake,
The thing that takes the cake,
Is the pride of all the place, the Village Pump.

The Village Pump, The Village Pump,
The Village Pump, Pump, Pump, Pump, Pump.
The Village Pump, The Village Pump,
The Village Pump, Pump, Pump, Pump, Pump.

One night the rummest chap you've ever seen,
Gave a temperance lecture on the village green.
He said us fellows here
Was much too fond of beer,
And he spouted like a penny magazine.
He damned The Cat and Fiddle and The Bull,
Till Jethro aimed a clout across his skull,
He said 'Water – that's for me!'
So we shouted, 'Right you be!'
And we took him out and ducked him in the pump.

The Village Pump, The Village Pump,
The Village Pump, Pump, Pump, Pump, Pump.
The Village Pump, The Village Pump,
The Village Pump, Pump, Pump, Pump, Pump.

We had a new policeman t'other week,
A sloppy-lookin' feller so to speak,
One that thought he was all there
But by gum I do declare
He was what you'd call a sort of livin' freak.
Martha Woodword says as how he's off his chump,
'Cause one night he came across a biggish lump,
And said: 'Move it, Joe, you're tight!'
But when he showed a light,
He found out he was talkin' to the Pump!

The Village Pump, The Village Pump,
The Village Pump, Pump, Pump, Pump, Pump.
The Village Pump, The Village Pump,
The Village Pump, Pump, Pump, Pump, Pump!

Answers to Quiz on page 59

1 A television set, and when he failed he hired one from a Borchester store and held a Coronation Party at his farm.

2 Clive Lawson-Hope, the ultra-smooth nephew of the Squire. He took Grace to the pictures and kissed her in the car on the way home, then he asked her to marry him, and while she was thinking about it he changed his mind and went after somebody else.

3 Bob Larkin, Ned's unmarried brother from Dorset, who came to Ambridge in 1957 and started making eyes at Tom's lady-love Pru, the bairmaid in The Bull. One night Tom was struggling in the woods when his gun went off and he discovered he had shot Bob dead. Tom was found not guilty of manslaughter at Gloucester Assizes.

4 New Street Station, Birmingham, in 1955. Jill was a kitchen appliance demonstrator in a city store.

5 Glebe Cottage – but only for Doris's lifetime. Dan and Doris retired to Glebe Cottage in 1970. In 1979 they bought the freehold outright but still in Doris's name, and she left it to Shula in her will.

6 In the West Indies. His wife Valerie and little daughter Hazel returned to Ambridge.

7 An elephant called Rosie, who had a baby called Tiny Tim. During the Ambridge Summer Festival (organised by John Tregorran) both elephants took part in a pageant depicting the Garden of Eden and were a huge success. Walter also had a pet parrot in 1965 (he acquired it playing Long John Silver in the 1964 village pantomime) but he gave it to Mrs Twelvetrees of Felpersham.

8 Roger Patillo, who used a false name because his family were cold and indifferent to him.

9 Toby Stobeman, a racing chum of Paul Johnson's.

10 Paddy Redmond, the Brookfield dairyman, who quarrelled with Phil over a milk bonus scheme and left the village before the truth could be revealed.

11 Nora McAuley. She married Greg Salt in 1968, later left him and lived with George Barford, and later still left George and moved in with a Borchester chap. She was last heard of working in the canning factory.

12 The cornet (with Hollerton Silver Band).

13 Gloucester Gaol, after conviction for an offence relating to the disposal of vast amounts of illicitly obtained copper piping.

14 Fish farming in the Am, a venture which came to grief when the filters became choked and thousands of little fishes died from lack of oxygen.

15 Eva Lenz who fell in love with, and was shamefully ill-used by, Nick Wearing. After he had gone she was ill-used a little bit by Eddie Grundy and then rescued by village policeman Jim Coverdale. They married and went to Devon.

16 The Prince of Wales's Own Regiment of Yorkshire.

17 Dolly Treadgold, in 1979. Joe put up new curtains in the parlour and prepared the turkey shed for the wedding reception, but Eddie called the wedding off because Dolly was too flighty.

18 John Tregorran. He was smitten when they compiled the Ambridge village survey together.

19 Simon Parker, the young editor of the *Borchester Echo*, in the autumn of 1977.

20 Nick Wearing, the son of a wealthy farmer who had spent several months at Brookfield gaining practical agricultural experience. Shula dumped him somewhere in the Far East, had her money stolen in Bangkok, and had to be flown home at Phil's expense.

21 Elizabeth, and Kate Aldridge.

22 Nelson Gabriel. In early 1971 he returned home after a mysterious trip abroad, bought Hollowtree Flats, and offered Lilian free accommodation if she would look after things for him. One night he made passionate advances, and she rejected him scornfully.

23 a) Tom and Pru
b) Jethro and Gyp
c) Pat, Tony and family
d) The Pargetter family. Lower Loxley House is affectionately known as 'Pargetter Hall'.
e) Neil, Susan, and Emma
f) Kathy Holland

24 a) Lizzie

b) Joby
c) Susan
d) George
e) Valerie

25 a) Jethro
b) Marjorie Antrobus
c) Pat and Tony

26 Three Blind Mice and The Teddy Bear's Picnic.

27 The Ritz.

28 A budgerigar called Joey.

29 An old record player.

30 Fallon.

31 Nigel Pargetter, who was thrown out of Pargetter Hall by his furious father, Gerald, after losing his job as a seeds rep.

32 Betty Tucker, who was offered the post when the Harveys moved to Singapore for six months. Mike had just been made bankrupt, and Betty was happy to have a job that would take her mind off things.

33 Marjorie Antrobus.

34 Jill Archer.

35 Neil Carter.

36 The Over Sixties. When she died Peggy took over.

37 He arrived late for work one day, without having had any breakfast, and helped himself to a slice of game pie from the Food Hall.

38 Phil and Jill, who were asked to dinner.

39 A remote-control telephone alarm in case he was taken ill.

40 Rick, a director friend of Hazel's.

41 The story of Noah's Ark.

42 Percy Jordan, who was doing the milking while Pat and Tony were enjoying a caravan holiday at Borth.

43 He grew a beard. Nobody liked it except for Sophie.

44 George Barford, who was accused of trapping wild mink with poison.

45 Lyme Regis. He took Lucy with him, and Kathy Holland drove them there and drove them back.

46 He refused to 'Die for the Queen'.

47 The lovely Lisa, famous for her lettuce soup.

48 Little wooden elephants.

49 Yo Yo (the group was called LeLuLus).

50 Wildlife Weekends to see 'Tarka of the Am'.

An Eddie Grundy Fan Club Christmas Card.

The Ambridge Story 1971-80

Walter campaigns vigorously against the closure of Ambridge village school. 1971 was a happy year for the Gabriels: Nelson was staying in luxurious Grey Gables while his penthouse flat was prepared at Hollowtree.

1971

Nelson attempted to seduce Lilian in his luxury flat at Hollowtree. She rejected him with scorn, but encouraged the shy advances of Squire Ralph Bellamy.

Jack Archer started working at Brookfield but collapsed with ill-health. After several weeks in Borchester General Hospital, doctors sent him to a sanatorium in Scotland.

Hugo Barnaby bought Nightingale Farm and turned it into a Centre for Rural Arts. He engaged Laura as assistant curator.

At Glebe Cottage Dan suffered from lumbago and Doris was baffled by decimal coinage. Dan built a large glass 'sun-lounge' extension. Tony Archer had a passionate romance with Roberta, who worked at Lilian's stables.

Jack Woolley went ahead with plans to turn part of his estate into a Country Park.

Lilian and Ralph Bellamy were married. Jack sent best wishes from his Scottish sanatorium. Ralph gave Lilian his superb horse Red Knight as a wedding gift.

Sid and Polly perks had a baby girl, and called her Lucy.

Sid and Polly out and about on a day trip to Boulogne. In December Polly gave birth to daughter Lucy. Hilary Newcombe (Polly).

A new landlord for The Bull – and a new pub sign. Poor Nora, though, was having a miserable year. After four years of marriage she had parted from Greg Salt. Julia Marks (Nora McAuley).

1972

Jack Archer died in the Scottish sanatorium. Peggy gave up running The Bull. She offered the tenancy to Sid and Polly. They accepted, and sold the shop to Jack Woolley.

Laura tried to buy 100 acres of Lakey Hill for a caravan site.

Tony had a passionate affair with a girl called Jane Petrie, neglected his work, and was sacked by Bellamy. He ran away to France for several weeks.

Jack Woolley opened a steam railway in his new Country Park. He and Dan went to Scotland to buy a steam engine and called it 'Empress of Ambridge'.

Tenant farmer Joe Grundy wooed Martha Lily, a widow from Penny Hassett, but she rejected him and married Joby Woodford.

An RAF trainer plane crashed near Heydon Berrow. The pilot baled out and landed in Borchester's sewage farm.

Jill had a nervous breakdown. She told Phil she could not carry on any longer and went to London. Christine looked after the children and Pru was taken on as a daily help at Brookfield. In November Jill recovered, and returned to Ambridge.

Tense times in Ambridge as Walter spots a poacher fleeing the estate with a rich haul. In December poachers stripped the coverts bare while Tom was dashing to Borchester after a hoax phone call saying that Pru was dangerously injured.

A brief moment of relaxation for Phil, as he sorts through his music for the Ambridge Folk Chorale. At Brookfield he was suffering from stress in 1973, and overwork caused him to crash his car on the way home from Borchester.

1973

The year of the Ambridge Festival. Dan was chairman, Phil organised a pop group, Doris organised the cottage gardens contest, and Jack Woolley underwrote the losses.

Barmaid Nora McAuley discovered that the new gamekeeper, George Barford, was an alcoholic.

Jack Woolley was in a coma for several days after being attacked by robbers at Grey Gables. Later in the year he collapsed with a heart attack when Valerie demanded a divorce. Peggy Archer took over the running of Grey Gables.

Sid Perks organised a village trip to Holland.

After threatening to close the village shop, Woolley engaged Martha Woodford as sub-postmistress.

A new farm apprentice, Neil Carter, started work at Brookfield and promptly mowed a field of ripening oats.

Joe Grundy spent some weeks in hospital with 'Farmer's Lung', collapsed outside The Bull with malnutrition, then crashed his lorry into the village pump and demolished it.

Tony Archer went into partnership with newcomer Haydn Evans at Willow Farm. He also fell in love with travelling farm secretary Mary Weston.

Lilian gave birth to a son, James Rodney Dominic.

Aunt Laura lost nearly all her money on the stock market and had to sack her companion, Miss Fairlie.

1974

Tony became engaged to Mary Weston and held a party in the new 'Ploughmans' bar at The Bull.

George Barford tried to commit suicide but was saved by Tom Forrest and Nora McAuley. Nora moved into his cottage with him.

After an outbreak of swine vesicular disease at Hollowtree, Phil's entire herd was slaughtered. Some of Dan's ewes were stolen from Lakey Hill and Phil started freeze-branding his cows to deter rustlers.

Neil Carter was put on probation for twelve months after police found drugs in his possession.

Opposite right: Peggy to the rescue! In 1973 she took over the running of Grey Gables after Jack Woolley had been clubbed by burglars, stricken by a heart attack, and threatened with divorce by Valerie.

Doris and Walter chat happily on the village green, but barmaid Nora McAuley wonders if she dares speak to them. Many villagers snubbed her when she became the mistress of alcoholic gamekeeper George Barford.

The drugs had been planted on him at a party by his girlfriend Sandy.

Shula started a secretarial course at Borchester Tech and became friendly with a much older man – hi-fi fanatic Eric Selwyn.

Joe Grundy opened a caravan site at Grange Farm and Walter Gabriel sent some tinkers to stay on it.

Mary Weston broke off her engagement to Tony. In the summer he met Pat Lewis, who proposed to him, and he accepted. They married in the autumn.

Bellamy was warned of heart trouble by his doctor and decided to sell most of his estate and retire to Guernsey.

Kenton Archer went to sea as a Merchant Navy cadet.

Jack Woolley proposed to Peggy but she turned him down and flirted for several weeks with a rogue interior designer called Dave Escott.

Bandits set up a road block and tried to attack the post-bus with iron bars.

Nora McAuley discovered she was pregnant by George Barford, quarrelled with him, moved back to The Bull, and had a miscarriage.

Newcomer to the village was Brian Aldridge, a rich 32-year-old bachelor who bought 1500 acres of the Bellamy estate.

Jennifer Travers-Macy left Roger and began divorce proceedings.

PC Drury accused Neil Carter of spraying paint over signposts and vandalising telephone boxes.

Polly Perks's father, arsonist Frank Mead, died in a mental hospital. Sid and Polly bought their 'dream cottage' in Penny Hassett for £4,500.

Joe Grundy won first prize with his marrows at the Flower and Produce Show.

On 31 December, Pat gave birth to a son, John Daniel.

Above: Lilian and Shula met Ann Moore the showjumper. Ann said that Shula showed promise as a competition rider, and Phil agreed to support her if she would also do a secretarial course at Borchester Tech. Liz Marlow (Lilian), Ann Moore, Judy Bennett (Shula).

Below: 'What a lad!' says Dan to a proud Tony who has just announced that Pat is expecting her first child in December. Edgar Harrison (Dan), Colin Skipp (Tony).

1976

Carol Tregorran was accused of shoplifting and found not guilty at Felpersham Crown Court. Doris and Christine were witnesses for the defence.

Joe Grundy won a luxury 'weekend for two' at Grey Gables, turned up alone, and demanded half the prize in cash.

Newcomer Brian Aldridge proposed to Jennifer and was accepted. They married at Borchester Registry Office. Brian bought Jennifer twelve Jacob sheep and she took up spinning.

Tom Forrest retired as full-time sporting manager at Grey Gables.

New arrivals were *Borchester Echo* editor Simon Parker, and Lt. Colonel Frederick Danby who became Laura's paying guest.

Jill collapsed and was rushed to hospital suffering from thyroid deficiency.

Neil Carter moved into a flat at Nightingale Farm, and fell in love with Shula. She, however, was more interested in *Echo* editor Simon Parker.

Woolley welcomes John Tregorran back from a lecture tour of America. The summer of 1975 also saw the brief return of Kenton: he brought Shula a grass skirt from Tahiti. Philip Morant (John Tregorran).

A candlelit dinner at Grey Gables for Jennifer Travers-Macy and the new owner of Home Farm, Brian Aldridge. In January he proposed, and they married as soon as her divorce was finalised. Angela Piper (Jennifer).

Woolley was horrified to find that Higgs was using his Bentley to visit his lady friend at Hollerton Junction.

Paul Johnson gave up an oil-industry job in London and returned to Ambridge. He admitted to an affair with a woman called Brenda.

1977

George Barford's son Terry mistook Joe Grundy for a poacher and hit him over the head.

The roof of Honeysuckle Cottage blew off, and Walter wandered round Ambridge for several weeks staying with friends.

Below: Tea on the lawn at Brookfield. Pat and Tony were glad to escape from Bridge Farm for a few hours: the Tuckers were lodging with them and driving Pat mad with their non-stop Country and Western music.

A happy smile from Tom, as he retired as full-time sporting manager. His cheeriness, alas, was short-lived. At Easter he started work at Woolley's new garden centre, and hated every minute of it.

Above: A happy smile from Sid Perks, who had just engaged a temporary barmaid, Caroline Bone from Darrington. Caroline promised to use her *cordon bleu* expertise to improve the bar food.

Below: A happy smile from Neil Carter, who survived the horrors of Weill's disease and went to a union convalescent home on the south coast. Brian Hewlett (Neil Carter).

Shula rode *Mister Jones* in the South Borset point-to-point at Scowell Braddon. She also went on a demonstration to stop Borchester Grammar School from going comprehensive, and was interviewed at length by Simon Parker. In the autumn they made love in a stubble field.

There was a bonfire on Lakey Hill to mark the Queen's Jubilee.

Paul Johnson started a new business venture – a fish farm. Tony and Pat took over the tenancy of Bridge Farm.

Adam was bitten by a viper on Heydon Berrow and only recovered after being treated with a new type of vaccine.

At The Bull, Sid took on a new temporary barmaid, Caroline Bone from Darrington, who had done a cordon bleu cookery course in Lausanne.

Jennifer gave birth to a daughter, Katherine Victoria.

Paul Johnson's fish farm was a disaster. Paul went bankrupt and disappeared taking Christine's car. He was eventually traced to Hamburg. He told Christine he was never coming back.

1978

Nora McAuley finally left George Barford and went to live with a man in Borchester.

Jethro's Uncle Charlie died and left him 'a fortune'. Clarrie gave up her cleaning job before she discovered the fortune was £4,200.

Shula found Joe Grundy delirious with flu and malnutrition at Grange Farm. Joe's singing-star son Eddie had abandoned him and gone to Hollerton with a floozie.

Jennifer and Brian built a swimming pool at Home Farm and engaged a German au-pair called Eva. Brian hit a work-shy employee and Jennifer threw a garden rake at union secretary Mike Tucker.

Shula was terribly upset when Simon Parker resigned from the *Echo* and moved to London.

Neil Carter was ill for several weeks with Weill's disease, picked up from touching rat's urine with a cut hand.

Despite village opposition Jack Woolley sold land to a builder for the 'Glebelands' development.

Jill and Jennifer started a craft stall in Borchester,

which they developed into a craft studio at Home Farm called the 'Two Jays'. The venture ended in disaster.

Eddie left his Hollerton floozie and returned to Grange Farm to start a turkey venture.

Paul Johnson was killed in a car crash in Germany. George Barford proposed to Christine and was accepted.

Pat and Tony took over the tenancy of Bridge Farm. The Brookfield cowman, Mike Tucker, and his wife Betty, moved to Willow Farm, and took over the partnership with Haydn Evans.

Right: The new barmaid at The Bull, Caroline Bone, soon introduced *cordon bleu* cooking to the Ploughman's. Sara Coward (Caroline Bone).

Below: Sunday lunchtime in The Bull, 1978. Walter had cause to look pleased with himself. His carved wooden animals were selling remarkably well at Jill and Jennifer's craft shop.

1979

Brian Aldridge shot a vixen that had taken several of his early lambs. Shula said he was no gentleman.

Christine and George were married in St Stephen's Church, despite the fact that George was divorced.

Pat gave birth to a daughter, Helen, who suffered for several months from a dislocated hip.

At Grange Farm Eddie became engaged to Dolly Treadgold, and Joe put new curtains up in the parlour. A reception was organised in the turkey shed and chicken legs and vol-au-vents ordered from The Bull. The day before the wedding Eddie called it off.

He said Dolly was too flighty.

Walter was taken to hospital suffering from sugar imbalance. Nelson came home from Venezuela, took his father off to Teneriffe, and they both returned to Ambridge penniless.

Shula went on a round-the-world trip but ran out of money in Bangkok. Phil had to telex funds to her and pay her hunt subscription when she returned.

Pat Archer ran away to Wales for two weeks and Tony worried about his marriage. When she returned she made him promise to relax more and work less.

Caroline Bone went to work at Grey Gables as Jack Woolley's 'Social Secretary'.

A new start for George Barford. Divorced from his wife in Yorkshire he married Christine Archer, and in the summer played a cornet solo at Hollerton Free Trade Hall. Graham Roberts (George Barford).

1980

Ralph Bellamy died in Guernsey after a heart attack. Lilian returned briefly to Ambridge and scandalised Peggy by drinking with Eddie Grundy.

John Tregorran fell in love with Jennifer while they were both doing a landscape survey of the village. When he tried to kiss her in Leader's Wood she fled from him.

Tony collapsed with tetanus poisoning and was dangerously ill for several weeks.

Shula started going out with a 26-year-old solicitor, Mark Hebden. At first she said he was boring, then she said she quite liked him. David Archer returned home from college and started going out with the notorious playgirl Jackie Woodstock, Shula's rival on the committee of Borchester Young Conservatives.

Jethro Larkin was horrified when his daughter Clarrie started walking out with Eddie Grundy. When Lizzie Larkin died he was ill with shock, and Clarrie agreed to stop seeing Eddie for a while.

Colonel Danby proposed to Laura, but she turned him down.

Nelson Gabriel ran up huge debts which Jack Woolley cleared on condition that Nelson left the village. He went to Borchester and opened a wine bar.

Above: A jolly moment with Granny Archer, as Pat and Tony prepare for the birth of their second child. Stormy times, however, were to lie ahead. Patricia Gallimore (Pat).

Below: At first Shula thought Mark Hebden was beautiful but boring. Then he flew to the rescue of a deer being attacked by dogs in the country park, and she decided he was a hero. Richard Derrington (Mark Hebden).

Above: Good times for Eddie Grundy. He was captain of the Cat and Fiddle darts team, had a well-paid job with Hollerton Plant Hire, and he was walking out with a respectable village girl, Clarrie Larkin. Trevor Harrison (Eddie), Heather Bell (Clarrie).

Left: After hearing sniggers and jokes about his relationship with Laura, Colonel Danby felt obliged to make an honest woman of her. He was relieved, however, when she turned down his offer of marriage. Ballard Berkeley (Colonel Danby).

7

Ambridge Gazetteer

Ambridge

Sweet Ambridge, loveliest village of the plain,
Where health and plenty cheered the labouring swain,
Where smiling spring its earliest visit paid,
And parting summer's lingering blooms delayed. . .

Oliver Goldsmith, 1756.

Ambridge is a village of some 360 inhabitants, six miles south of Borchester on the B3980. Its buildings are a mixture of thatched black-and-white timbered cottages, and houses in mellow brick and stone. Few buildings date from later than Victorian times. Exceptions include six old-people's bungalows and a small development of high-quality houses.

The River Am runs through the village, and behind it the ground rises to Lakey Hill and beyond that to the Hassett Hills. From the summit of Lakey Hill you can see across the Vale of Am to the Malverns, and, on a clear day, to the distant mountains of Wales. The village has a pond (with ducks), a village green, and a fine wooden bus shelter. There is no bus service, however, other than the school bus. There is a pub, shop, and village hall. Most of its inhabitants work in farming or commute to Borchester or Felpersham.

Ambridge Farm

For many years Ambridge Farm was a 150-acre tenant within the Bellamy Estate, occupied by Ken and Mary Pound. When Ken died the tenancy was given to Mike and Betty Tucker who also ran a milk round – bottling their own 'green top' milk – and tried to run a farm shop. Mike went bankrupt in the winter of 1985 and the land was absorbed back into the estate. The Tuckers continued to live in the farm-house, paying a minimal rent, until 1986 when it

was bought by Matthew Thorogood the new village doctor.

Ambridge Hall

For many years Ambridge Hall was the residence of Laura Archer – 'Aunt Laura' – and her paying guest Colonel Danby. When Laura died the property was inherited by her niece in New Zealand, and Freddie stayed on as a tenant until the house was sold in the summer of 1986. It is a Victorian edifice which must have been an eyesore in the 1860s when it was built (by Squire Lawson-Hope as a home for the doctor). Now, though, the yellow bricks and green tiles have mellowed, there are attractive wooden shutters on the windows, and mature beech and willow trees in the garden. It is a large house and difficult to heat properly in the winter. The grounds contain a rather good glass sunhouse, and outhouses which were used for keeping goats, ducks, hens, and pet lambs when Laura and Freddie were the occupants. There is a splendid fruit garden, and the lawns run down to the River Am. The hall is now the home of computer programmer Robert Snell and his wife Linda.

Blossom Hill Cottage

The home of Peggy Archer since she left The Bull in 1972. Before then it was occupied briefly by young Sixties-mad Tony Archer who let hippies sleep on the floor and entertained girls at scandalous hours; and before Tony lived there it belonged to John Tregorran. The cottage has two bedrooms, and a pleasant sitting-room with french windows leading out to the garden. In 1982 it was burgled by Ben Warner (Shula caught him on the job) and a year later it was badly

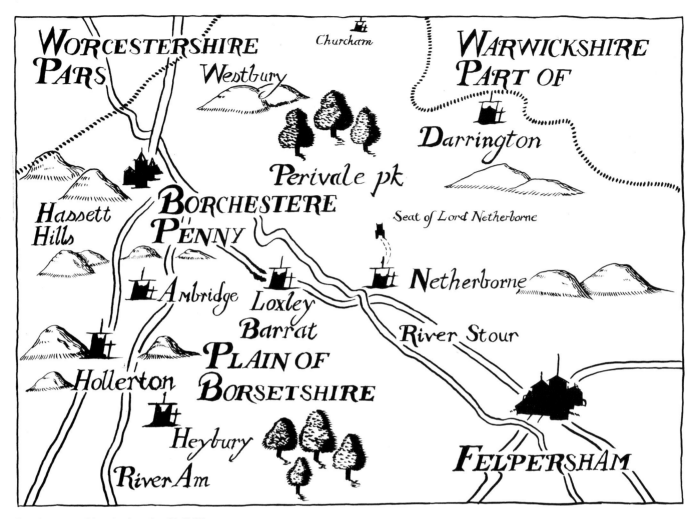

South Borsetshire during the Civil War.

damaged by fire. Apart from Peggy, the cottage is occupied by Sammy the cat.

Borchester

A market town of some 15,000 inhabitants, six miles north of Ambridge. Its history can be traced back to Roman times, when it was an important staging post on the road (now the A1999) from Akeman Street to Droitwich. The town has a Magistrates' Court, cinema, and some notable riverside gardens by the Am. There is a thriving livestock market (Thursdays). The traditional 'mop' fair is held on the first Thursday and Friday after Michaelmas. Educational establishments include the High School (Comprehensive), the South Borsetshire Technical College, and Borchester Grammar School (Independent school for boys and girls).

Bridge Farm

A tenant farm (140 acres) on the Bellamy estate, farmed by Tony and Pat Archer. The farmhouse is late-Victorian red-brick and totally undistinguished. It has traditionally been a dairy farm, devoted to grassland and a small acreage of barley, but in late 1984 Tony and Pat decided to 'go organic' by cutting out artificial fertilisers, herbicides, and pesticides on their land. In 1985 they grew ten acres of organic wheat, carrots, and potatoes; and each year are continuing to devote more of their land to organic production. Pat Archer also keeps around 100 hens on a free-range system.

Brookfield Farm

Despite a recent sale of land, Brookfield still extends to over 450 acres and is very much a traditional 'mixed' farm, with cows, pigs, sheep and corn. The old, mellow brick and timber farmhouse dates back to the sixteenth century, and is in the centre of one of Ambridge's four medieval open fields (West Field, Lakey Hill Field, East Field, and Brook Field). The farm has been in the hands of the Archer family for five generations, first as a tenanted farm and then purchased freehold in the late fifties. It is now farmed by Phil and Jill Archer, with their son David. The dairy herd numbers around 100 Friesians and there are around 80 followers. There is a pig unit, and a flock of 300 ewes (mainly a cross-breed known as 'mules'). Round the farmhouse at Brookfield there are usually a couple of dozen free-range hens. Also working the farm are Graham Collard (cowman) and Jethro Larkin (general).

The Bull

A black-and-white timbered hostelry dating for the most part from the late seventeenth century, although the back of the building is said to be older – a ghost who 'taps' on a back-bedroom window is reputed to be that of a drummer boy from the Civil War. The pub faces the village green and is a freehouse owned by Mrs Peggy Archer. The licensee is Sid Perks. There are two bars, the Public and the Ploughman's and there is a 'snug' (next to the Public Bar) and an upstairs function room containing a rather ancient piano. The Bull sells the highly acclaimed Shire's best bitter, a traditional ale from the Borchester Brewery. Food is served both at lunchtime and in the evening, and is mainly of the snack variety (bread and cheese, hot pies and pizzas, chicken or scampi and chips). There are five guest bedrooms, although the bed-and-breakfast trade is mainly confined to the summer. The Bull has a darts team (Winter League) and there is keen rivalry every December when the local derby is played against the team from The Cat and Fiddle at Edgeley.

The Cat and Fiddle

A public house of ill repute just outside the hamlet of Edgeley on the A1999, opposite Wharton's Garage, and the turning to Ambridge. The landlord is Dick Pearson. The darts team includes Winter League stars such as 'Snatch' Foster, 'Bugsie', and 'Foxy' Sugden. The Christmas darts match between The Cat and Fiddle and The Bull is a social event.

The Bull

Council Houses

On the far side of the Village Green, next to Manorfield Close, the twelve council houses are semi-detached and each has a good vegetable plot and flower garden. The Horobins live at No. 1, and No. 6 ('Dunroamin') is occupied by Neil and Susan Carter and their daughter Emma.

Country Park

Ambridge Country Park is part of the Grey Gables estate and runs from Grey Gables itself down to the River Am. There are woodland trails and a small information centre (not manned). The park has deer in it and includes Arkwright Lake.

Darrington

A village some twenty miles from Ambridge on the Warwickshire border. The ancient blue-back Hassett sheep now survive only in the Darrington

Rare Breeds Centre. Caroline Bone's family live in the Manor House.

Domesday Ambridge

Borsetshire comes towards the end of the first folio of the Domesday Book. The entry for Ambridge reads: 'The Prior of St Mary's, Worcester, holds Ambridge with one berewick. Eadred holds it of him. There are ten hides. There are four ploughlands in desmesne with 8 serfs. Eight villeins, 12 bordars, and 2 cottars have 12 ploughs. There is woodland 3 leagues by half a league and five acres of meadow. There is a mill rendering 200 eels annually. In the time of King Edward it was worth 80 shillings, and is now 100 shillings.' NOTE: The amount of recorded woodland seems surprisingly large in relation to the known extent of woodland in the parish at a later date, and it may be that Ambridge had an interest in woodland resources well outside the present parish – perhaps in the Forest of Am.

Dower House

An eighteenth-century house built at the same time as Ambridge Manor, the home of the Lawson family, which no longer exists. The Dower House was the home of Ralph and Lilian Bellamy before they moved to Guernsey.

Edgeley

A hamlet on the A1999, just by the turning to Ambridge. Mary Pound lives in a bungalow at Edgeley.

The Feathers

A seventeenth-century hotel in Borchester, now owned by Trusthouse Forte. The Lounge Bar is a popular lunchtime meeting place for farmers on market day. Borchester Rotary Club meets here every Wednesday.

Felpersham

A city, about the size of Worcester, some seventeen miles from Ambridge. Felpersham has a repertory theatre, Crown Court, large department stores and some fine shops including Laura Ashley, Austin Reed, and Habitat.

Glebe Cottage

Built around 1840, Glebe Cottage is a small house of mellow bricks south of the village and next to St Stephen's Church. It was left to Doris Archer 'during her lifetime' by her former employer, Lettie Lawson-Hope. Dan and Doris later bought the freehold from the Lawson-Hope family and retired there when they left Brookfield. It has a fine glass conservatory built in 1970 and a classic English cottage garden. Glebe Cottage was left to Shula Archer by her grandmother, and when Dan died Shula and Mark moved in and carried out extensive renovations.

Glebelands

A development of eight modern houses, each with four bedrooms, two bathrooms, and a patio. The small estate is opposite Glebe Cottage and St Stephen's church. The nearest house to the road is occupied by the Fletcher family.

Glebe Cottage

Goat and Nightgown

Borchester's bohemian pub, close to the Technical College, which also (surprisingly perhaps) provides a home for Borchester Country and Western Club. It is a pub of nooks, crannies, and dark corners. Pat Archer used to meet her sociology lecturer Robert here of an evening after 'Women's Studies' at the Tech.

Grange Farm

Built on eighteenth-century foundations, Grange Farm is a mixture of stone, crumbling brick, and cement rendering which is cracked, stained, and falling away from the front wall of the house in chunks. There is an old solid-fuel stove in the kitchen, which also has an orange plastic-tiled floor, an old-fashioned enamelled kitchen sink, brown-painted cupboards on the walls, and a glass-fronted 'kitchenette' unit bought in 1958. The farm is rented from the Bellamy Estate by Joe Grundy, who works the farm with his son Eddie and daughter-in-law Clarrie. Eddie has converted the cellar into a Country-and-Western shrine, and has painted herds of bison (crossing the plains of Wyoming) on the walls. Outside the house is an area of ground that Clarrie struggles every year to turn into a garden. There is also a turkey shed where Joe raises around fifty turkeys every autumn, and where Grange Farm celebrations used to be held in days gone by. It was last decked out with bunting in 1979 when Eddie was getting married to Dolly Treadgold (the wedding was called off and the party cancelled). The farm covers 120 acres. There are around 35 Friesians in the dairy herd, and between 15 and 20 followers depending on the general financial state of the farm.

Grey Gables

Grey Gables Country House Hotel is owned by former Birmingham businessman Jack Woolley, who also owns a large part of Lyttleton Covert, the Country Park, a garden centre, and a small golf course with its own club house and bar. Grey Gables itself is a late-Victorian Gothic mansion set in fifteen acres of lawns and gardens. The parkland is noted for its fine chestnut trees. The house has twenty-four bedrooms (each with private bathroom), a restaurant, cocktail bar, lounge bar, and banqueting hall. There is a ground-floor 'Royal Garden Suite' named (quite

Grange Farm

improperly) to mark the visit to Grey Gables by HRH the Princess Margaret. Staff at Grey Gables includes a chef called Jean-Paul (famous for his French tartlets), assistant restaurant manageress Trudy Porter, and Higgs the handyman. The Ambridge cricket pitch, with clubhouse, is on Grey Gables land donated by Jack Woolley, and there is an outdoor swimming pool at the hotel.

Heydon Berrow

Once an area of common land, to the south of the village, that was absorbed into the Lawson estate in the mid-seventeenth century. When he was thirteen Adam Macy had the misfortune to fall off his pony on Heydon Berrow and be instantly bitten by an adder.

Hollerton

A large village three miles south of Ambridge on the B3980. Hollerton was a rival village to Ambridge in the eighteenth century:

> The Hassett boys are very good boys
>   The Hollerton boys are better,
> The Ambridge boys can stand on one leg
>   And kick them in the gutter.

The prosperity and growth of Hollerton in the nineteenth century was due to the arrival of the Great Western Railway which connected to the local Midland line at Hollerton Junction. The small village grew rapidly, and Hollerton Free Trade Hall still stands as a memorial to those expansionist times.

Hollerton Junction

Just over two miles south of Ambridge, Hollerton Junction is on the Inter-city Hereford-Paddington line. Trains usually take around two hours ten minutes to reach London, although the introduction of faster 125 trains in 1984 has provided one slightly speedier 'up' and 'down' train each day. There used to be a splendid restaurant car on the 8.06 am and 9.06 am trains to London, but this service was scandalously withdrawn some years ago.

Hollowtree

Once one of four, small, self-contained working farms spread along the valley of the Am. Now only Brookfield remains in its own right and the others (Sawyers, Wynfords, and Bull Farm) have been absorbed into larger units. As a result many hedges and boundaries have disappeared. Hollowtree farmhouse was occupied by Phil and Jill Archer for a short time, but the building was later abandoned and then converted into the Brookfield Pig Unit. It now houses sixty sows producing offspring that are sold as baconers. There are four boars at the Unit, and the senior one is always known as 'Playboy'.

Home Farm

Covers 1,500 acres and is mainly arable, although there is a flock of 600 ewes (200 lambing in January; 400 in March and April) and a beef unit. Cereals dominate the farm's economy – 900 acres of wheat and barley, and a substantial acreage of oilseed rape. Working the farm with Brian Aldridge are Steve Manson (foreman), Sammy Whipple (cattle and sheep), three tractor drivers and one boy. The farmhouse is built on the foundations of the ancient Lyttleton Manor, and is principally early eighteenth century in origin. After the Second World War it was converted to superior luxury flats and the land round it was farmed as part of the Bellamy Estate. It was converted back into a house by Brian Aldridge in 1975.

Honeysuckle Cottage

To the north of the Village Green, not far from the pond and on the opposite side of the road from the Village Hall, Honeysuckle Cottage is a black-and-white thatched building with an old English garden. It has a living-room and kitchen downstairs, and a bedroom and bathroom upstairs. It is the home of Walter Gabriel, and has been for many years. In the mid seventies his son Nelson (then an entrepreneur in London) had the loft discreetly boarded so that he could store strange packages and crates in it.

Jiggin's Field

A Romano–British site on the lower slopes of Lakey Hill next to the Borchester road. The site was partly excavated in 1975–6 due to the threat of deep ploughing (See *Transactions of the Borsetshire Archaeological Society, Vol. LXVIII*). The site was revealed as a farmstead comprising several ranges of timber buildings including both domestic accommodation and agricultural ranges, within a ditched rectangular enclosure, occupied from the second to the fourth century AD.

Keeper's Cottage

One of two estate cottages built in the mid Sixties by Ralph Bellamy, Keeper's Cottage lies in the valley of the Am between Leader's Wood and Willow Farm, and is the home of Tom and Pru Forrest. Next to it is April Cottage occupied by Martha Woodford.

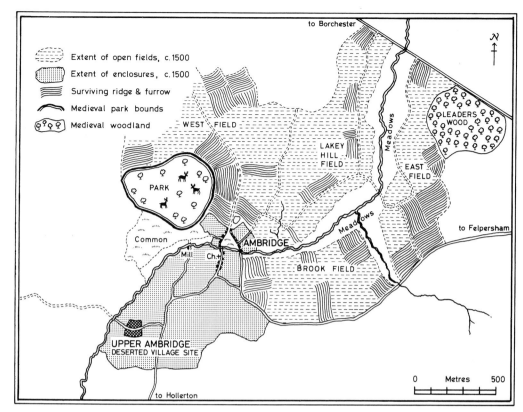

Legend:
- Extent of open fields, c.1500
- Extent of enclosures, c.1500
- Surviving ridge & furrow
- Medieval park bounds
- Medieval woodland

Map labels: to Borchester, WEST FIELD, LAKEY HILL FIELD, LEADERS WOOD, Meadows, EAST FIELD, to Felpersham, PARK, Common, AMBRIDGE, Mill, Ch., BROOK FIELD, Meadows, UPPER AMBRIDGE DESERTED VILLAGE SITE, to Hollerton, 0 Metres 500

Medieval Ambridge

Lakey Hill

Immediately north of Ambridge, Lakey Hill's southern slopes and summit are included in Brookfield land and are used to graze sheep. Near the summit is a group of three barrows or burial mounds of Bronze Age date, although these have been much reduced by ploughing since the Second World War, and are now about a metre high. A bonfire has been lit on Lakey Hill every Midsummer's Eve since Tudor times, and bonfires have also been lit to mark coronations and royal jubilees. The bonfire to celebrate Queen Victoria's jubilee in 1887 was lit by Dan Archer's father; he himself was in charge of the victory bonfire of 1919, and Phil Archer has vivid memories of the bonfire that was lit on the eve of the Queen's coronation in 1953. In more recent times, Shula Archer was on the committee which organised the jubilee bonfire of 1977, on which occasion Lakey Hill was part of the official chain laced across the kingdom, joining Clee and Malvern to Edge Hill and the beacons of the south.

Loxley Barratt

A village four miles east of Ambridge on the Felpersham road.

Manor Court

A fine eighteenth-century gentleman's house on three acres, and the home of Carol and John Tregorran. Near the house is a one-acre vineyard which produces the well-established Manor Court wine.

Manorfield Close

On the far side of the village green, beyond the duck pond and shielded behind an evergreen hedge, Manorfield Close is a small development of old folks' bungalows. No. 2 is occupied by Mrs Perkins, and No. 3 by Mrs Bagshawe. In 1986 Colonel Danby also became an occupant of the close.

Medieval Ambridge

The village had a deer park (where the deer park is now), a church and a mill, and an area of ancient woodland at Leader's Wood. Documentary evidence shows that the parish had four open fields: West Field, Lakey Hill Field, East Field, and Brook Field.

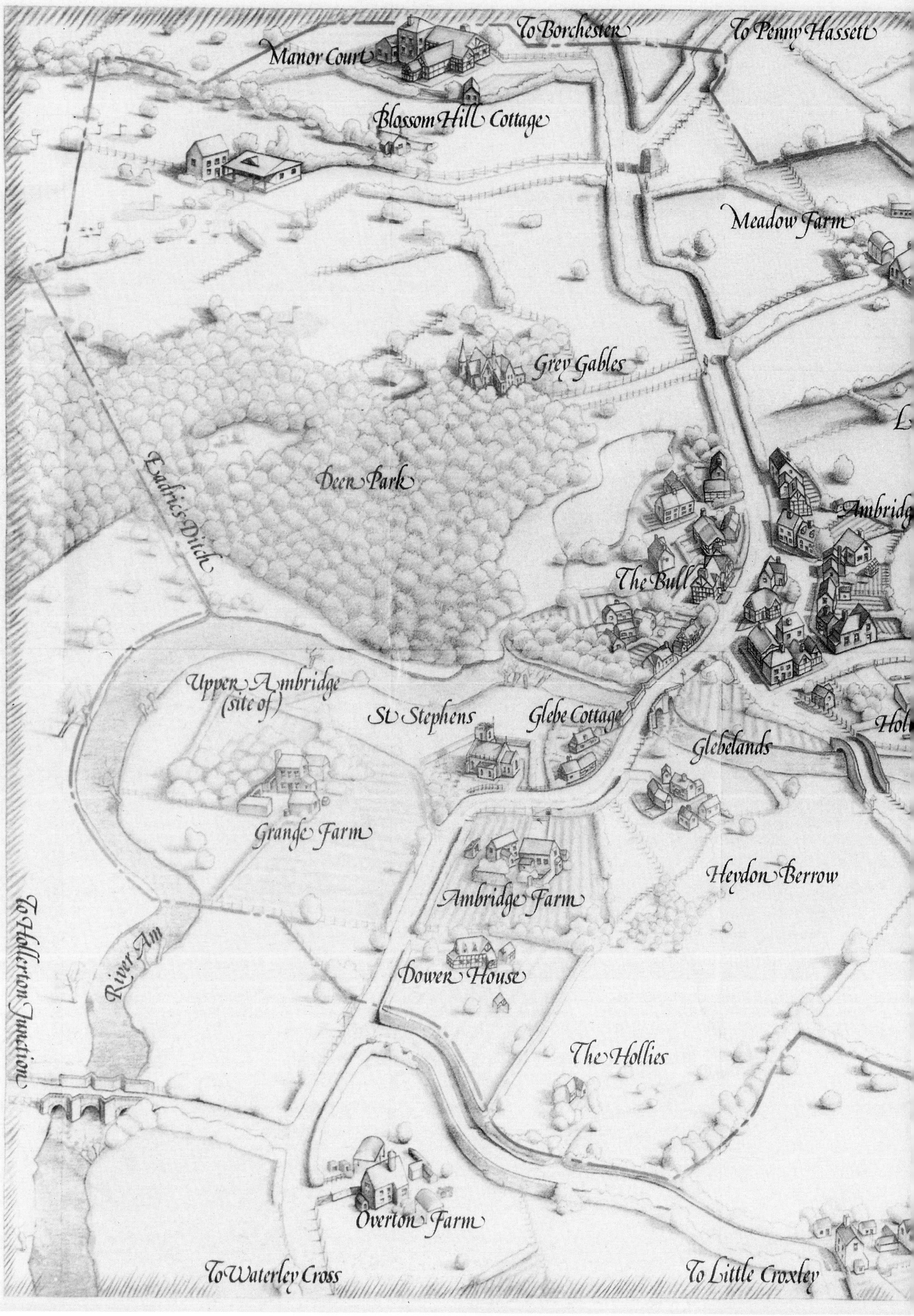

Manor Court

To Borchester

To Penny Hassett

Blossom Hill Cottage

Meadow Farm

Grey Gables

Eadries Ditch

Deen Park

Ambridge

The Bull

Upper Ambridge
(site of)

St Stephens

Glebe Cottage

Glebelands

Hol

Grange Farm

Heydon Berrow

River Am

Ambridge Farm

To Hollerton Junction

Dower House

The Hollies

Overton Farm

To Waterley Cross

To Little Croxley

Iron Age Fort

To Penny Hassett

To Edgley

Hassett Hill

Lyttleton Bridge

Paved Street

Lyttleton Cover

Three Barrows

Roman Road

Willow Farm

Leaders Wood

Marneys Farm

Ambridge Hall

Home Farm

River Am

Brookfield Farm

Oak Wood

Traitors Ford

Bridge Farm

Ten Elms Rise

To Felpersham

Heath

Oak Farm

Parish Boundary

N

To Little Croxley

Nelson's

A bar in West Street, Borchester, owned by Nelson Gabriel. It was formerly a wine bar, but renamed a cocktail bar in 1985. There is food available, provided by Shane the chef. Above the bar is Nelson's flat. The bar is connected by an open archway to the next-door antiques shop, also run by Nelson.

Netherbourne

A village six miles east of Ambridge. The Hall is the home of Lord Netherbourne, who is related to Caroline Bone, and who now lives in the East Wing of the house and hires out the rest for conferences and wedding receptions. Shula and Mark Hebden held their reception here in September 1985.

Nightingale Farm

Set back from the Netherbourne and Loxley Barratt road, Nightingale Farm was used as a rural Arts and Crafts Centre until 1975, and then for several years as a village youth club. The building included a two-bedroomed flat, and this was occupied by Neil Carter and various of his friends, male and female. When Neil married Susan Horobin in 1984 they lived in the flat until the owner, Hugo Barnaby, offered a cash inducement for them to give up the tenancy. They moved into a council house on The Green and Nightingale Farm was bought by Mrs Marjorie Antrobus, a breeder and shower of Afghan hounds. Mrs Antrobus restored the downstairs of the farmhouse to its original state, and converted the outbuildings into excellent kennels for her dogs.

Penny Hassett

The closest village to Ambridge, on the north side of Lakey Hill. It is somewhat larger than Ambridge. The pub is The Griffin's Head. Sid Perks owns a cottage in the village, Rose Cottage, which he and Polly bought as an investment in the late Seventies. When Kathy Holland moved to the area she rented it from him on an annual basis. As a village, Penny Hassett has always had a strong community spirit. On Plough Monday (the first Monday after Twelfth Night) the start of the farming year is celebrated by drawing a plough decorated with green and yellow ribbons (representing grass and corn) through the village street. On Shrove Tuesday there is a traditional pancake race organised by the WI.

Police House

Built in brick in 1931, the Police House was sold by Borsetshire Constabulary after PC Coverdale left the village. It was bought by Det. Sgt. David Barry, who promply had pine-cladding fitted to one wall of the kitchen and painted the rest of it canary yellow.

Rodway and Watson

A firm of estate agents in Borchester. Shula Archer worked there for several years before moving to the Bellamy Estate. Mr Watson is no more, and it is Mr Rodway who runs the business. The office is in the High Street.

Roman Ambridge

Apart from the Romano–British site at Jiggin's Field, a landscape survey of Ambridge in 1981 yielded finds of Romano–British materials at Home Farm and at the site of Sawyer's Farm. The Ambridge area was colonised by the Romans from AD 46 onwards, some three years after the invasion of Britain under Emperor Claudius. From the time the XIV Legion crossed the line of what is now the Fosse Way, to the end of the fifth century the county was a settled and prosperous part of the Roman Empire. The administration of the area was based on the tribal capital of the Dubunni at Cirencester (Corinium).

Rose Cottage

A small cottage in Penny Hassett owned by Sid Perks and rented to Kathy Holland from 1983 until their marriage in 1987.

Saddler's

An old-fashioned restaurant-cum-tea room in Borchester which also sells high-quality foodstuffs and gourmet delights. The set lunch of soup, roast-and-two-veg and steamed pudding for afters has not changed (except in price) for three generations.

The Stables

Some distance from the centre of the village, the Stables comprise a nondescript brick-built house with riding stables and an indoor riding school (built when the business was owned by Lilian Bellamy). The Stables were bought by Ambridge Farmers as a home for Christine Johnson after her husband Paul died in 1978. She married gamekeeper George

Barford the following year, and they now live in the house.

St Stephen's Church

The present church was built on the site of an early seventh-century St Augustine church, and was consecrated in 1281. Architecturally it is a combination of Saxon, late Norman, and early English and Perpendicular styles.

The **chancel** has a fine example of a priest's doorway (eleventh century) in the south wall. The north wall is early thirteenth century, the south is fifteenth century, and the east is a mixture of both. Also in the chancel are two fifteenth-century benches.

The **altar** of stone was added to the church in 1842 and the heads were carved to match those on the font.

The **font** is octagonal and is contemporary with

St Stephen's Church

the rest of the church. It is of carved stone, very ornate and enriched with carved human heads and flowers. It is believed to have been a gift to the church by Edward I and two of the heads are thought to be those of the King and Queen Eleanor of Castille.

The **nave** has an early thirteenth-century north arcade. The windows, one in the west wall and one west of the porch in the south wall, are both late fourteenth century.

The **Lawson Chapel** (or South Transept) was added in the early sixteenth century. The Lawson family bought the Manors of Ambridge and Lyttleton in 1472 and during the reign of Henry VII Richard Lawson depopulated Lyttleton and enclosed the Manor Farm lands to the east of the parish.

Until 1934 there were three **chained books** in the church, but these are now held in safe custody by Borsetshire Country Record Office. The Record Office also holds the church registers from 1599 to 1837. The valuable church silver is lodged in the bank and includes an Elizabethan chalice with cover.

Several of the gravestone inscriptions in Ambridge church and churchyard show the work of rural poets through the centuries.

> All you that do this day pafs by,
> As you are now, fo once was I,
> As I am now fo fhalt you be,
> Therefore prepare to follow me.
>
> Ed. Blower, 1710

> Here lie Paul and Richard Fenn,
> Two lawyers, yet two honest men.
> God works miracles now and again.
>
> 21 June 1746

> My anvil and hammer lies declined,
> My bellows have quite lost their wind,
> My fire's extinct, my forge decay'd,
> My vice is in the dust all laid.
> My coals is spent, my iron gone,
> My nails are drove, my work is done,
> My mortal part rests nigh this stone,
> My soul to heaven, I hope is gone.
>
> Thomas Salter, Blacksmith of
> Ambridge, d. 12 June, 1784.

The vicar of Ambridge (who is also rector of Penny Hassett and vicar of Edgeley) is Richard Adamson. The churchwardens at St Stephen's are Tom Forrest and Jill Archer. The monthly parish magazine is edited by Mrs Antrobus.

Ten Elms Rise

A small but prominent hill west of the village. In the Seventies there were only two elm trees left on the hill, and both of these were killed by Dutch Elm Disease.

Underwoods

The only department store in Borchester, well known for its excellent food hall.

The Vicarage

A modern four-bedroomed house occupied by the Rev. Richard Adamson, his wife Dorothy, and their two children Rachel and Michael (when they are home from college).

Victorian Ambridge

In 1850 the *History, Gazetteer and Directory of Borsetshire* listed Ambridge as:

A parish and pleasant village five miles south of Borchester. It contains 2,210 acres of land. In 1841 there were 79 houses with 394 inhabitants. The rateable value was £2259. In 1803 the parish rates were £441.11.2d at 6s.6d in the pound. The abbot of St Mary's, Worcester, was an early possessor of the lordship, which now resides with the Lawson–Hope family. A carrier calls on Thursday from Hollerton to Borchester, and returns.

Directory
Blower T., Baker and miller
Box R., Shoemaker
Clarke T., Shopkeeper
Hands R., Hurdle-maker
Morris J., Schoolmaster
Mumford R., Carpenter
Perrin S., Publican and maltster
Rev. Richard Leadbeater, Vicar
Slatter J., Carpenter
Gabriel J., Blacksmith
Waters C., Farrier
Rouse J., Wheelwright

The village in 1850 milled the corn grown in its own fields, baked its own bread and brewed its own ale. It made its own furniture and tools, its carts, field-gates, coffins and cribs, its boots and its smocks. Children were taught at the village school and the village church. With the exception of the squire, vicar, and schoolmaster, everyone in the village lived on the land or by one of the trades associated with it – blacksmith, wheelwright, farrier, hurdle-maker, bootmaker and carpenter.

Village Hall

Built in 1920 as a memorial hall to those who died in the Great War, the Village Hall is principally used by the Playgroup (run every morning, Monday to Friday, by Dorothy Adamson and helpers) and by the Over Sixties, who meet here once a week. The hall is run by a sub-committee of the Parish Council.

Village Shop

Owned by Jack Woolley, the shop is run by Martha Woodford. Dorothy Adamson also helps part-time. The shop sells mainly foodstuffs, tobacco, sweets, newspapers and magazines. There is also a post office counter. The shop closes for lunch between 1 pm and 2 pm. Half-day closing is on a Thursday.

Waterley Cross

A large village some five miles south of Ambridge on the B3991.

Wharton's Garage

A garage on the main A1999 Borchester road, close to The Cat and Fiddle and opposite the turning to Ambridge. The bus from Borchester to Hollerton stops here, leaving passengers with a walk of 1½ miles down into Ambridge village.

Willow Farm

Formerly a 100-acre farm on the slopes of Lakey Hill, the land was divided between Brookfield and Home Farm in the early Eighties, and the farmhouse and a few acres were bought by Bill Insley. The farmhouse itself is an unattractive red-brick building with ivy covering the front wall. For some time Neil Carter used a couple of old farm buildings for his battery-hens and deep-litter birds, and in the winter of 1985 he joined in a pig venture with Bill Insley. In the summer of 1986 Bill Insley died of a heart attack. In his will Neil was left enough land and buildings to continue with the pig venture.

Woodbine Cottage

The home of Jethro Larkin, Woodbine Cottage is owned by Ambridge Farmers. It is in the centre of the village, next to The Bull and overlooking the Village Green.

8

The Ambridge Story 1981-87

In his best bootlace tie Eddie contemplates married life and Joe thinks of all the chicken legs and mushroom *vol-au-vents* he's had to pay for. Haydn Jones (Joe).

A flustered Clarrie arrives at the church in a minibus which she had to share with Jethro, Eddie, and Joe.

Married at last!

A brave smile from Jethro, after giving away his daughter to the terrible Grundys.

1981

Doris Archer died. In her will she left Glebe Cottage to Dan during his lifetime, and then to Shula.

Jill became active in the WRVS and ran a holiday scheme for deprived city children.

Pat Archer gave birth to a son, Tommy.

Shula and Mark became engaged, bought a cottage in Penny Hassett and started to renovate it.

Nelson opened an antiques shop next to his wine bar and persuaded Lilian to invest in it.

Former SAS officer Alan Frazer rented 'The Lodge' and nearly broke Tom Forrest's arm when he caught him snooping. He had a love affair with Caroline before mysteriously leaving the village.

Clarrie Larkin and Eddie Grundy were married. Alf Grundy was best man.

Shula had a brief, deep, and meaningful relationship with Ben Warner of Penny Hassett then broke off her engagement to Mark.

Nelson shows his new antiques shop to Caroline. He had reason to smile: as an extra sideline he had Clarrie, Joe, and Eddie bottling herbal shampoo in the Grange Farm turkey shed. Jack May (Nelson).

1982

Neil Carter became engaged to Julie, the barmaid at The Bull, and she moved into Nightingale Farm with him.

Eddie disappeared to London for several weeks, doing 'gigs' with Jolene Rogers and Wayne Tucson. He returned penniless and Clarrie forgave him.

Polly Perks was killed when her car was in collision with a milk tanker.

Haydn Evans decided to sell Willow Farm and move back to Wales. The Tuckers were on the point of being evicted when they were offered the tenancy of Ambridge Farm.

Pat developed strong leftist leanings, started attending a 'Womens' Studies' course at Borchester Tech, and had an affair with a sociology lecturer called Roger.

Clarrie went to Great Yarmouth to look after her sister Rosie, and gave birth to a son, William, in a Great Yarmouth hospital.

Shula stumbled across a burglar in Blossom Hill Cottage. It was her friend Ben Warner from Penny Hassett. After days of anguish she told the police.

Sid conducts the raffle at the Ambridge Fête. In the autumn of 1982 the Perks family was dealt a tragic blow when Polly was killed in a road accident leaving him to bring up their only child, Lucy.

Caroline proudly shows Shula her horse, Ivor, which she brought over from Darrington and stabled at Grey Gables.

1983

Neil Carter was abandoned by Julie the barmaid who ran away to London.

Eddie and Joe were banned from The Bull after Eddie had been sick in the pub piano.

Joby Woodford died. Martha tried to contact his spirit through a Borchester 'medium'.

Hazel Woolley paid a long visit to Grey Gables. She amused herself by seducing Tony and then telling him to get lost. Then she sacked Higgs for impertinence. Jack had to give him a big pay rise to get him back.

Bill Insley, a retired Derbyshire farmer, bought Willow Farm and started to chat up Martha Woodford.

Village girl Susan Horobin won a piglet called Pinky at the fête. Neil helped her look after it and became her friend.

Nigel Pargetter appeared on the Ambridge scene. At the opening meet of the South Borset hunt he fell off his mount and was carried to Brookfield where he fell in love with Shula.

Caroline went to Scotland to the Edinburgh Festival and Nelson went with her to escape from his creditors.

Above: As the year came to an end Nigel Pargetter fell off his horse in Phil's barley, frightened Tom Forrest witless by dancing through the Country Park in a gorilla outfit, drank champagne out of Jack Woolley's Dahlia Society Challenge Cup, and encouraged New Year revellers to run amok at Grey Gables. Graham Seed (Nigel).

Below: An unrepentant Eddie Grundy, banned from The Bull after being sick inside a piano.

Elizabeth was expelled from boarding school for offences that involved boys, drinking, smoking, and wearing her uniform in an incorrect manner. She came home and happily signed up to do her A levels at Borchester Tech.

1984

Pat and Tony began organic farming at Bridge Farm.

Joe Grundy and Bill Insley spent many weeks competing for Martha Woodford's company and steamed jam puddings.

Susan and Neil were married.

Jack Woolley fell off the roof of Grey Gables and was unconscious in hospital for several days. Hazel returned to Grey Gables, poisoned the goldfish with vodka and kicked Captain. Nigel Pargetter called her a 'she-wolf'.

Susan Carter gave birth to a baby girl, Emma, who was kept in hospital for some time suffering from jaundice.

Nigel (sleeping on the Brookfield sofa) sought Shula during the night, went into the wrong bedroom, whispered 'tally-ho' and jumped into bed with Phil.

Princess Margaret attended an NSPCC gala dinner at Grey Gables, as did the Duke of Westminster. Jack was astounded to discover that the Duke and Caroline were old friends.

Nigel was found guilty of taking and driving away a sports car; Shula, who was with Nigel at the time, was defended by Mark and was found 'not guilty'. Shula realised she still loved Mark and was devastated when he went off to Hong Kong for a year.

Elizabeth was expelled from her boarding school and started going out with Nigel. Shula started going out with the new young vet Martin Lambert.

Terry Barford was seriously injured in a road accident in Berlin. The army flew his father out to Germany to be with him.

1985

Laura Archer died. Her will, leaving Ambridge Hall to Freddie, was unsigned, and the property was inherited by Laura's niece, Judy Cameron, living in New Zealand.

Shula stopped going out with vet Martin Lambert and flew to Hong Kong to see Mark. He followed her back to England, re-proposed to her on Lakey Hill, and they were married in September.

Nigel lost his job selling swimming pools and was sent to Africa by his family. He returned with little wooden elephants for everyone. In the summer he worked as Mr Snowy the Icecream Man.

Jill became the local organiser for Meals on Wheels.

Caroline had a romance with a Sea-Harrier pilot from Yeovilton.

Right: Jack Woolley chooses a spot for the Grey Gables swimming pool. He was finalising the deal with Nigel Pargetter when he spotted Captain out on the rooftops, went to rescue him, and fell head first into a flowerbed. He was seriously ill for several weeks. Arnold Peters (Woolley).

Below: Shula phones Mark in Hong Kong. She's coming out East for her holiday. Can he look after her?

The Tuckers went bankrupt at Ambridge Farm.

Hazel Woolley became Conference Organiser and PRO at Grey Gables and made a promotion video of the hotel that cost thousands of pounds.

Neil decided to leave Brookfield and join Bill Insley in a pig venture.

David started going out with student fashion designer Sophie Barlow.

Below: Bridesmaids Kate Aldridge and Elizabeth Archer at Shula and Mark's wedding reception at Netherbourne Hall.

10 DOWNING STREET

The Prime Minister, the Rt Hon Margaret Thatcher, FRS, MP, and Mr Denis Thatcher convey their thanks to Mr and Mrs Philip Archer for their kind invitation to the wedding of their daughter Shula Mary to Mark Hebden but regret they are unable to attend.

19 September 1985

Right: Brian keeps his eyes – and clearly his thoughts – on Caroline Bone. When her Sea Harrier pilot betrayed her he moved in and rekindled their smouldering affair. Tony found them kissing in a cornfield and dining at the exclusive *Mont Blanc* but failed to realise what was afoot.

Above: Tony enjoys the bracing air of Borth. He would rather have gone on holiday to Crete, but Pat preferred her native Wales.

Below: A new girlfriend for David. After Jackie Woodstock and Virginia Derwent he started going out with fashion-design student Sophie Barlow.

Nigel tells Lizzie terrible tales about his adventures in Africa.

1986 to Spring 1987

Dan Archer died in May of a heart attack trying to right a ewe which had fallen on her back. Nelson Gabriel's illegitimate daughter turned up in the wine bar ... only Walter did not doubt that she was Nelson's daughter, as he had known Nancy Tarrant was pregnant nineteen years before.

David Archer became engaged to Sophie Barlowe as they watched the Royal Wedding in July.

Caroline Bone had a riding accident and was examined by Matthew Thorogood, a handsome young locum. Their romance began and Matthew joined Dr Poole's practice and opened a branch surgery in Ambridge.

The Tuckers moved out of Ambridge Farm to make way for Matthew, and lived temporarily in The Bull while they searched for accommodation. Eventually Betty Tucker became Jennifer Aldridge's homehelp and the family moved into a tied cottage on Home Farm.

Colonel Danby also moved house, from Ambridge Hall to one of the old people's bungalows in Manorfield Close. The Hall was bought by the Snells from Sunningdale, a couple who had made their fortune with their own computer business.

Elizabeth Archer passed only one of her 'A' Levels, attempted to set up her own fashion business with Sophie Barlowe and was forced to take a nine-to-five job selling advertising space on the *Borchester Echo* to pay off her debts. Phil found himself in debt as well – to the taxman. Dan's death created a tax bill of £50,000.

Walter Gabriel tried to make Nelson queue all night to buy him a heated hostess trolley in the sales.

Brian Aldridge bought a race horse, 'Two Timer', and tried to renew his affair with Caroline Bone.

Mike Tucker took a course in woodland management and Jennifer Aldridge provided him with a chain saw.

Richard Adamson ruffled the feathers of his flock by suggesting the sale of postcards in the church.

Shula became land agent for the Bellamy Estate. She stayed away from Brookfield's aborting ewes when she thought she was pregnant.

David and Sophie's romance suffered from her absence in London as a fashion designer. She went out with Nigel Pargetter and David was very hurt.

Elizabeth took up with Robin, Grace Fairbrother's half-brother. Jill could not bring herself to meet him.

Lucy Perks was unhappy when Sid and Kathy Holland became engaged.

Joe Grundy put an advert in a Lonely Hearts column and received two replies. One was from the dog-woman, Marjorie Antrobus, and the other was from Sandra, who has a twelve-year-old son called Jason. Eddie and Clarrie were worried.

Phil sold a parcel of land to help meet his tax bill.

Sid Perks and Kathy Holland were married in Borchester Registry Office.

Right: Phil likes Sophie – he's even prepared to show a lively interest in her textile designs.

Below: Lizzie has got an A level – and Nelson suggests champagne.

9

The Villagers

DOROTHY ADAMSON works part-time in the village shop and helps to run the playgroup. She is married to Richard Adamson, and they have two children, Rachel and Michael, who are in their early twenties.

RICHARD ADAMSON is the vicar of Ambridge and rector of Penny Hassett. He and his family moved to Ambridge in 1973. A strong advocate of Series Three Communion, he agreed to marry Christine and George in church even though George was divorced.

BRIAN ALDRIDGE bought Home Farm in 1975 after his parents had been killed in a car crash and the family farm in the Home Counties had been bought for building development. He was educated at Sherborne School and has one sister, Liz, who is married to a stockbroker and lives in Cheshire. In the early-Eighties Brian had an affair with Caroline Bone, and in 1987 bought a racehorse called 'Two Timer'. The same year he introduced deer to Home Farm.

JENNIFER ALDRIDGE is the eldest child of Peggy and Jack Archer, and was born in 1945. She trained as a teacher and had two novels published while still in her twenties. In 1966 she had an illegitimate baby, Adam. She married Roger Travers-Macy and they had a daughter, Deborah, but the marriage was not a success and they were divorced in 1976. She married Brian Aldridge the same year, and they have one child, Kate. Jennifer writes the weekly woman's page for the *Borchester Echo*.

MARJORIE ANTROBUS first appeared in Ambridge in 1983 when she addressed the Over Sixties on 'The Colourful World of the Afghan'. A noted dog breeder, she bought Nightingale Farm in 1985, and for a time Nigel Pargetter was her lodger. She is editor of the parish magazine.

DAVID ARCHER was nicknamed 'Snowball' as a child because of his blond hair. Educated at public school he went on to study at the Royal Agricultural College, Cirencester, and then spent a year on a farm in Holland. After a series of racy girlfriends (including Jackie Woodstock and the notorious Virginia Derwent) he became engaged to Sophie Barlow in July 1986. By 1987, however, Sophie had moved to London to work for a fashion house and the romance seemed to be heading for the rocks. The same year he applied for the job of manager of the Bellamy Estate.

Brian Aldridge

Jill, David and Elizabeth Archer at Brookfield.

ELIZABETH ARCHER was rushed into hospital soon after birth for a series of 'hole-in-the-heart' operations. After failing the 11-plus she was sent to boarding school where she learned the piano and flute and campaigned to 'Save the Whale'. She was expelled from school after developing a friendship with Nigel Pargetter, and did her 'A' levels at Borchester Tech. She passed in only one, English, in 1986. After a summer season as 'Miss Snowy' the ice-cream maid she ended up selling advertising space for the Borchester Echo. In 1987 she became involved with Robin Fairbrother, the half brother of her father's first wife.

JILL ARCHER met Phil at the Ambridge Fête in 1957 and he proposed to her at New Street Station, Birmingham, three months later. They were married on 16 November. The following year Jill gave birth to twins, Kenton and Shula. In 1959 came David, followed by Elizabeth in 1967. Jill has been a member of the Parish Council and the Rural District Council, and is an active supporter of the WRVS. She was a member of the committee which fought to stop Borchester Grammar from going independent when Borsetshire's education system went comprehensive. She has been a quiet but steady opponent of bloodsports. In 1986 she baled Elizabeth and Sophie out when they tried to go into the fashion business. She was deeply upset by Elizabeth's involvement with Robin Fairbrother.

Pat Archer

PAT ARCHER came to Ambridge in 1974 to look after her Uncle Haydn. She met Tony, and they were married before the end of the year. On 31 December 1975 she gave birth to a son, John Daniel, and in 1979 she had a daughter, Helen. In the early Eighties she developed interests in left-wing politics, attended 'Women's Peace Group' meetings in Borchester, and changed the family's daily newspaper from the *Express* to the *Guardian*. In 1984 she had an affair with a sociology lecturer called Roger. The feminist pantomine she attempted to produce in the village in 1986 did not get off the ground.

PEGGY ARCHER was born in the East End of London and was brought up as a non-conformist and a socialist. She met Jack Archer during the War when she was a stores orderly in the ATS. They married and ran a small-holding for several years before taking over The Bull. Jack's weakness for argument, gambling and drink grew worse over the years, and it was largely left to Peggy to run the pub and bring up their family – daughters Jennifer and Lilian, and son Tony. When Jack died she left The Bull and now lives in Blossom Hill Cottage with her cat Sammy, and helps out at the Bellamy Estate Office.

PHIL ARCHER went to the village school and in 1939 won a place at Borchester Grammar. After the War he went to a Farming Institute and then became farm manager for Mr Fairbrother. In 1955 he married Grace Fairbrother and they lived in Coombe Farmhouse. In September 1955 she died after a stables fire at Grey Gables. Two years later Phil met and married Jill Patterson, a store demonstrator. They have four children, Shula, Kenton, David, and Elizabeth. The family moved into Brookfield Farm in 1971 when Dan and Doris retired. Phil is a church organist, plays the piano rather well, is a magistrate, and a member of the PCC. He was forced to sell land at Brookfield when faced with a tax bill of £50,000.

SHULA MARY ARCHER was born in 1958, the twin of Kenton. From an early age she was passionately interested in horses, and until her late teens had the ambition to become a show jumper. When she realised she was not sufficiently talented she joined estate agents Rodway and Watson, sat her 'A' levels at Borchester Tech, and took a professional 3-year course in valuation and estate agency. She was social secretary of Borchester Young Conservatives for many years. In 1980 she became engaged to Mark Hebden, but broke off the engagement a year later. In the summer of 1985 she asked Mark to take her back, and they were married in September. When Dan died they moved into Glebe Cottage. The following year she took over the running of the Bellamy Estate. In the spring of 1987 she thought she was pregnant.

TONY ARCHER was christened Anthony William Daniel and is the only son of Jack and Peggy Archer. His sisters, both older than he is, are Jennifer and Lilian. After leaving school Tony went to the Walford Farm Institute in Shropshire and then worked as a farm manager on the Bellamy estate. In the early Seventies he worked for a time at Brookfield. In 1973 he went into partnership with Haydn Evans at Willow Farm and became engaged to farm secretary Mary Weston. Mary called off the engagement after only a few months, and in December 1974 Tony married Pat Evans, his partner's niece from Wales. In 1978 they took over the tenancy of Bridge Farm and in 1984 began the gradual change to organic farming.

CHRISTINE BARFORD is the only daughter of Dan and Doris Archer, and after attending Borchester Grammar School became an outside milk sampler for the Ministry of Agriculture. A noted beauty in her youth, she married handsome, rich, horse-owner Paul Johnson. Although the marriage lasted over 20 years much of it was unhappy, mainly due to Paul's business failures. When his final business – a fish farm – collapsed in 1977 he went bankrupt, left Christine and went to Germany where he was killed in a car crash. Christine moved out of their home, and her brother Phil bought the riding stables for her. In 1979 she married George Barford. She has one son, adopted, called Peter. She was responsible for training Brian's racehorse, 'Two-Timer'.

GEORGE BARFORD came to Ambridge in 1973 as assistant keeper at Grey Gables. Previously he had been a policeman in Yorkshire, and had split up from his wife Ellen in 1970. A reformed alcoholic, he tried to commit suicide in 1974, and was saved by Tom Forrest and Nora McAuley. After a long affair with Nora he eventually married Christine, and they now live at The Stables. George's son, Terry, is an NCO in the Prince of Wales's Own Regiment.

DAVE BARRY is a police sergeant whose hobby is bird watching. He became closely involved with Ambridge life in 1983 when he investigated the disappearance of the Over Sixties' tea money. Soon after, he bought the old Ambridge police house. The following year he became friendly with Lucy Perks's school teacher, Kathy Holland, and spent a lot of time trying to persuade her to live with him. In 1986 he sat his inspector's exam and failed. His romance with Kathy Holland also ended.

LILIAN BELLAMY is Peggy Archer's younger daughter and was born in 1947. After school she qualified as a riding instructor, and a year later met and married a Canadian Air Force pilot called Lester Nichols who died in hospital in 1970. Her second husband was the village 'Squire', Ralph Bellamy, who died from a heart attack at their Guernsey home in 1979. Lilian still lives on Guernsey, together with her son James, who will eventually inherit what remains of the Bellamy Estate.

CAROLINE BONE came to Ambridge in 1977 as the temporary live-in barmaid at The Bull. In 1980 she moved to Grey Gables as Jack Woolley's personal assistant, and has successively introduced *nouvelle cuisine* and classic English cooking to the restaurant. She is distantly related to both Lord Netherbourne and the Duke of Westminster, and her younger brother, Tim, is a captain in the Queen's Own Hussars. She had an affair with Brian Aldridge but called it off and started going out with newcomer Doctor Matthew Thorogood.

NEIL CARTER came to Brookfield as a sixteen-year-old 'new entrant' farming apprentice in 1973. After lodging with Martha Woodford he moved into a flat at Nightingale Farm. In 1984 he married a village girl, Susan Horobin, and they moved to a council house facing the Village Green. For many years he ran a small battery-hen egg business, and in 1986 he left Brookfield – where he was in charge of the Pig Unit – to breed pigs in partnership with Bill Insley at Willow Farm. After Bill's death he continued to keep pigs in the buildings left to him in the will. He works part-time at Brookfield.

SUSAN CARTER grew up in a council house on The Green with her terrible 'Horobin brothers' – Keith, Stuart, and Gary – and her little sister Tracy. In 1983 she started working full-time behind the bar in The Bull and the same year won a pig (called Pinky) at the church fête. Neil Carter helped her look after it, and in due course they were married and Susan gave birth to a little girl, Emma Louise. Susan helps out at The Bull, leaving her mum to look after Emma.

LIEUTENANT COLONEL FREDERICK DANBY retired from the army in 1976 and became the Borsetshire and Gloucestershire area rep-resentative for a national charity. He first came to Ambridge when he answered Laura Archer's advert for a paying guest at Ambridge Hall. In the following years he and Laura dabbled in 'self-sufficiency' and kept a succession of animals which included Edric the pig (eaten by Freddie and Laura), Heidi the Goat (eaten by a passing lynx), Jessica the hen (rescued from Neil Carter's battery house) and numerous ducks. When Laura died 'Freddie' stayed on in Ambridge Hall until it was sold by Laura's niece. He now lives in one of the Old Folk's bungalows at Manorfield Close where he had to ward off the solicitous attentions of his female neighbours.

PRU FORREST was thirty years old when she became friendly with vigorous gamekeeper Tom Forrest back in 1956. Two years later they were married, and unable to have children of their own they fostered two boys, Johnnie Martin and Peter Stephens. Nowadays Pru is famed for her sloe gin, her cakes and puddings, and for winning a great number of prizes at the annual Flower and Produce Show.

TOM FORREST and his sister Doris (who married Dan Archer of Brookfield Farm) were the children of gamekeeper George Forrest, and after leaving school at thirteen Tom followed in his father's footsteps and began a working life of ceaseless warfare against predators and poachers. He was charged with manslaughter after killing Bob Larkin during a midnight scuffle in the woods, but cleared at Gloucester Assizes. After a long courtship he married Pru Harris, the barmaid at The Bull, and they fostered two children, Johnnie and Peter. In 1976 he went into semi-retirement and for a while he and Pru ran the Grey Gables garden centre. He was not happy, though, and soon resumed his job as a gamekeeper, part-time.

NELSON GABRIEL is the only child of Walter and Annie, and after doing national service in the RAF he became a slightly mysterious 'businessman'. In the mid Sixties he opened the Borchester casino with Toby Stobeman. In May 1967 he was reported dead after a light plane crashed over the coast of France, but two months later his fingerprints were found on an empty whisky bottle in the hide-out of the Borchester Mailvan robbers. Tracked down by Interpol, he stood trial for armed robbery and other

Tom Forrest

members of the gang testified that he had been known as 'The Boss'. Despite the evidence he was acquitted. In 1980, after many years property speculating in London, he returned to Borchester and opened a wine bar and later an antiques shop. In 1986 he discovered that he had a daughter, Rosemary, the result of a moment of passion with Nancy Tarrant of Penny Hassett in 1967. He was involved in a housing development on Brookfield land in 1987 acting as the agent for a mysterious third party.

WALTER GABRIEL was born in 1896, the son of the village blacksmith. He was made a widower in 1934 when his wife Annie died and left him to bring up their only child, Nelson. After many years as a small tenant farmer he retired in 1957 and took up a variety of activities, including a pig venture and a maggot-breeding business. In 1977 he was homeless for many months when the roof of Honeysuckle Cottage had to be replaced, and in 1979 he was seriously ill in hospital suffering from a sugar imbalance. He has been friendly with Mrs Perkins ever since she moved to the village, and has proposed to her several times.

CLARRIE GRUNDY came to Ambridge in 1966 when her father Jethro Larkin got a job as general worker at Brookfield Farm. When she grew up her dream was to be an airline hostess, and for a time she worked at a travel agent's in Borchester. After that she was the daily help at Brookfield, and barmaid at The Bull. In 1980 Eddie Grundy asked her out for a chop-suey in Borchester's Woo-Ping restaurant and they started to walk out together. When her mother died she inherited £500 insurance money. She agreed to spend some of it on a demo record for Eddie providing the remainder was spent on an engagement ring. Eddie accepted the bargain. They were married in 1981, and have two sons, William and Edward. She continues to work part time at The Bull and attempts to keep the Grundy tribe in good order and clean underwear.

EDDIE GRUNDY was born in 1951, the younger son of Joe and Susan Grundy, tenant farmers of Grange Farm. He went to the village school and then to Borchester Secondary Modern, during which time he used to kiss and cuddle Lilian Bellamy in the back of the school bus. In 1979 he was briefly engaged to divorcee Dolly Treadgold, and after that he tried to seduce Eva the au-pair, was hit over the head in The Bull, and accused of theft by his employers, Hollerton Plant Hire. In 1980 he sang 'The Cowboy's Farewell to his Horse' at the vicar's 'Songs of Praise' in Ambridge Church. He is married to Clarrie and they live at Grange Farm with sons William and Edward, and Eddie's father, Joe Grundy. He has made three Country and Western records, and is the leading light of the Borchester C & W Club.

Nelson Gabriel

JOE GRUNDY is the son of George Grundy, who was given the tenancy of Grange Farm when he came back from Palestine in 1919 and became a famous cricketer in the Borchester Minor League. Joe took over the tenancy in the early Fifties and farmed with his wife Susan and their two sons Alfred and Edward. Susan died in 1969. In 1978 Alf left the farm to go scrap-metal dealing in Gloucester (he ended up in gaol), and Eddie disappeared off with a blowzy blonde from the Borchester bus station cafeteria leaving his father delirious with flu. Then half the herd went down with brucellosis and his favourite ferret Turk was found dead in a trap. Life only improved when Eddie returned, married Clarrie Larkin, and brought her to Grange Farm to cook

them all proper dinners. He has written two chapters of an autobiography called *A Straight Furrow, by Joe Grundy, 'Man of the Land'* which is designed to expose the way his father was cheated out of the Brookfield tenancy while he was away fighting the First World War. In 1987 he put an advert in the Lonely Hearts Column and had two replies.

MARK HEBDEN went to Shrewsbury School, read Law at Durham University, and qualified as a solicitor in 1977. His parents live in Borchester and his mother, Bunty, is a flower arranger of renown. In 1981 he was engaged to marry Shula Archer but she called the wedding off and in the following two years he had a long affair with Jackie Woodstock, inherited £25,000, considered becoming a blacksmith, and was engaged to solicitor's daughter Sarah Locke. In 1984 he went to Hong Kong for a year, and Shula flew out to join him for a holiday. They again became engaged, and were married in September 1985. When Dan Archer died they moved into Glebe Cottage. He is an SDP member of Borchester Council.

KATHY HOLLAND teaches home economics at Borchester Grammar School, where she was Lucy Perks's form mistress. She was married but separated from her husband. She seemed very close to Sid Perks at one time, but in 1985 started to go out with Dave Barry – a relationship which lasted for over a year. She took up with Sid Perks again and they were married in April 1987 in the face of Lucy's opposition.

MARTIN LAMBERT is the assistant vet at Bill Robertson's practice in Borchester, and has responsibility for routine herd visits in the Ambridge area. In 1984 he went out with Shula Archer for several months.

NIGEL PARGETTER is the only son of Gerald and Julia Pargetter of Lower Loxley House, Loxley Barratt, and in his day was a leading light of the Borchester Young Conservatives. In 1983 he fell in love with Shula but in the following year he was banned from Brookfield when, on the night of the Hunt Ball, he crept into Phil and Jill's bedroom having supposedly mistaken it for the bathroom. Later that year he was convicted of taking and driving away a sports car which he thought belonged to Tim Beecham (it didn't). Shula gave him the push and he

Joe Grundy

started going out with Elizabeth. He got sacked from selling swimming pools and Elizabeth chucked him. His family sent him to an uncle in Zimbabwe and he returned after a few weeks.

In the summer of 1985 he was 'Mr Snowy' and drove an ice-cream van, and in the autumn he sold toffee-apples at Borchester Fair. In 1986 he went off to London to work for a City stockbroking firm.

MRS PERKINS is the mother of Peggy Archer. She came to Ambridge when she was widowed in 1951, returned to London after marrying her 'second Perkins' and came back when widowed yet again. For several decades she has been amorously pursued by Walter Gabriel. She lives in one of the Old Folk's bungalows in Manorfield Close, next door to Mrs Bagshawe and not far from Mrs Potter.

SID PERKS is landlord of The Bull, and has one daughter, Lucy. He first came to Ambridge in 1963 as a callow teenager from Birmingham. He married Polly Meade and they kept the village shop before taking over the pub after the death of Jack Archer. Polly was killed in a road accident in 1982, and Sid was left to bring up Lucy on his own. In 1987 he asked Kathy Holland, one of Lucy's teachers, to marry him. She accepted, and the wedding took place in April.

MARY POUND now lives in a bungalow at Edgeley, but for many years she and her husband Ken were the tenants of Ambridge Farm. Ken died in 1983 after a long illness. Their daughter Marilyn is married to postman Harry Booker.

CAROL TREGORRAN still runs the market garden she started in 1954 when she came to Ambridge from Surrey and bought a smallholding off Dan Archer. Her name then was Carol Grey, and she caused a stir in the village by driving her own car. In 1963 she married businessman Charles Grenville, and after his death two years later she married John Tregorran (who had been courting her ever since she arrived in the village). In 1975 she was acquitted on a shoplifting charge. She and John own a small vineyard producing Manor Court wine.

JOHN TREGORRAN appeared in Ambridge after winning £12,000 on the football pools and resigning from his teaching job in a university. He instantly fell in love with Carol Grey, but she rejected him in favour of businessman Charles Grenville. In 1963 he married district nurse Janet Sheldon who died soon after in a car crash. He and Carol (now widowed) married and bought Manor Court, where they now live. He had a brief romantic infatuation with Jennifer Aldridge in 1981. Much of his time is spent travelling and lecturing on antique English furniture.

Sid Perks

money to buy back and run the milk round in her name. After being forced to leave Ambridge Farm they were given a cottage by Jennifer Aldridge and Betty worked as her housekeeper/home help, while still working as a part-time barmaid at 'The Bull'.

MIKE TUCKER was dairy manager at Brookfield and local secretary of the Farm Workers' Union when Haydn Evans offered him a partnership at Willow Farm. He and his wife Betty became farmers in their own right, and in 1982, when Willow Farm was sold, they took over the tenancy of Ambridge Farm. Despite their hard work Mike was forced to declare himself bankrupt in January 1986 having over-borrowed from the bank. The family lived in the farmhouse at Ambridge Farm, ran the local milkround, but were forced to move. Mike eventually took a course in Woodland Management.

MARTHA WOODFORD used to be Martha Lily, and her husband Herbert was the Penny Hassett postman. In 1961 Herbert died and Martha moved to Ambridge where she eventually took over the running of the village shop. Her second husband, Joby, died in 1983.

HAZEL WOOLLEY is the only daughter of Reggie and Valerie Trentham, and was born in 1956. She spent her early life in the West Indies, but when her father died her mother brought her back to Ambridge. Valerie's second marriage was to Jack Woolley, who adopted Hazel as his daughter. She now lives in London and works (so she says) as a PA in the film industry. To Woolley's disappointment she rarely comes to visit him.

JACK WOOLLEY came to Ambridge in 1962, a self-made man from Stirchley in Birmingham who bought Grey Gables Country Club and planned to turn it into an 'exclusive holiday centre for tired business executives'. In due course he married Valerie Trentham (Reggie had died in the West Indies) and adopted her daughter Hazel. His marriage to Valerie did not last, and since his divorce he has proposed to Peggy several times. He owns the village shop, the *Borchester Echo*, and the Borchester Press. His great interest is now the growing of chrysanthemums, and his loyal companion is his dog Captain, a Staffordshire bull terrier. He is a supporter of the cricket team and the Over Sixties Club.

BETTY TUCKER was born in 1950 and came to Ambridge in 1973 when her husband Mike became dairy manager at Brookfield. In 1978 she gave birth to a son, Roy, and in 1981 to a daughter, Brenda. By this time the family had moved to Willow Farm, where Mike had a partnership with Haydn Evans. In 1983 they were given the tenancy of Ambridge Farm, but ran into financial trouble and Mike declared himself bankrupt early in 1986. Betty then raised

10
The Cast

The Archers cast collecting the Sony Radio Gold Award which was presented to the longest running daily radio serial, May 1987.
1 Judy Bennett (Shula), 2 Graham Roberts (George), 3 Timothy Bentinck (David), 4 Richard Derrington (Mark), 5 Charles Collingwood (Brian), 6 Tracy-Jane White (Lucy), 7 Moir Leslie (Sophie), 8 Alan Devereux (Sid), 9 Margot Boyd (Mrs Antrobus), 10 Charlotte Martin (Susan Carter), 11 David Vann (Det. Sgt. Barry), 12 Jack May (Nelson), 13 Carole Boyd (Lynda Snell), 14 Nigel Caliburn (Nigel), 15 Colin Skipp (Tony), 16 Lesley Saweard (Christine), 17 Fiona Mathieson (Clarrie), 18 Alison Dowling (Elizabeth), 19 Terry Molloy (Mike Tucker), 20 Sara Coward (Caroline), 21 Arnold Peters (Jack Woolley), 22 Ballard Berkeley (Col. Danby), 23 Edward Kelsey (Joe), 24 Trevor Harrison (Eddie), 25 Angela Piper (Jennifer), 26 June Spencer (Peggy), 27 Bob Arnold (Tom), 28 Norman Painting (Phil), 29 Patricia Greene (Jill), 30 Pauline Seville (Mrs Perkins), 31 Chriss Gittins (Walter).

BOB ARNOLD (Tom Forrest) was born on Boxing Day, 1910, in the Cotswold village of Asthall, which lies in the Windrush Valley half-way between Minster Lovell and Burford. He didn't make much progress at school (so he says) and when he was fourteen he started work for a butcher in Burford and was paid five shillings a week.

'My father kept the village pub at Asthall, known then as the "Three Horse Shoes", but sadly it didn't make enough profit to support us,' Bob says. More troubles came in 1932 when he was taken seriously ill and spent fifteen months in hospital with a tubercular spine. 'When I came out of hospital the only job I could get was painting white lines on roads for Oxfordshire County Council.'

In 1939 Bob got his big chance in broadcasting. A programme called 'In the Cotswolds' was being made, and as Bob was well-known round Burford as a young singer and 'teller of stories' he was invited to take part. That led to other BBC Midlands programmes, and he soon found himself being billed in variety shows as 'Bob Arnold – the Farmer's boy!'

After the war, which he spent in the RAF, he started to get steady work on Children's Hour and in radio drama, and then, in 1950, he auditioned for The Archers and was told: 'You'll never be used by us because you've such a recognizable accent.'

There was a change of heart, though, and some four months later he was offered the part of Tom Forrest. He's been playing it ever since, and for over thirty years he introduced the Sunday omnibus.

HEATHER BARRETT (Dorothy Adamson) was so amazed when she first came to Pebble Mill to act in The Archers, to be working among voices that she'd 'grown up with from being a little girl' that she forgot her cue. Now she's married to Terry Molloy (Mike Tucker) she hears an Archers voice at home as well!

Heather trained at the Northern School of Music and Drama in Manchester, and had her first acting job at Oldham Rep before moving on to Manchester's Library Theatre. She has toured with Brian Way's Theatre Centre Co. and done an enormous number of radio plays for the BBC in Manchester and Birmingham.

'As you may know life in this profession is not an unbroken line of work, work, work,' says Heather, 'and in "resting" phases I have filled in with lots of different things – mostly selling, you name it, I've sold it!'

Once, she says, she dressed up as a fat, fluffy, yellow chick in an Egg Marketing Campaign, and knocked on peoples' doors very early in the morning to ask what they'd been eating for breakfast.

She also works from time to time as a television researcher. She and Terry have two sons, Robert and Philip.

JUDY BENNETT (Shula Archer) was educated at a Liverpool convent grammar school, and made her first public performance when she was fourteen, playing St Bernadette at a festival in the Philharmonic Hall. After studying at the Guildhall School of Music and Drama she got her first job as an ASM and understudy in *The Chinese Prime Minister* at the Globe Theatre – only to be sacked for not having an Equity card. She did a walk-on part in 'Emergency Ward 10', got her union card, and returned to The Globe as ASM/understudy in *The Cavern*.

In 1966 she auditioned for BBC Schools Radio, and was given her first radio job by Richard Wortley, playing a boy. More radio work rapidly followed, including parts in 'The Dales' and 'Waggoner's Walk'. In June 1971 she joined 'The Archers' to play Shula – and she specializes in children's voices to such an extent that she has also successfully played brother Kenton, sister Elizabeth, and Adam Travers-Macy!

Her voice is often heard (though not always recognized) on television, where she has brought to life characters in puppet series and cartoons like 'Rupert the Bear', 'Mumfie', 'Cloppa Castle', 'The Munch Bunch', and 'The Perishers' – and on radio she presented the pre-school radio programme 'Playtime' for nine years.

She has also taken lead roles in many radio plays, including Pip in *Great Expectations* and David in *David Copperfield*.

Judy is married to Charles Collingwood (who plays Brian Aldridge) and has three children.

TIMOTHY BENTINCK (David Archer) is one of the few members of the cast with any practical experience of agriculture, having been born on a sheep station in Tasmania ('My parents emigrated there but came home for some conversation'), and worked on farms for pocket-money all through his childhood. He recently took time off to help his father renovate and stock a smallholding in Devon, and he's delivered twin lambs in a snowstorm on New Year's Eve and hand-milked a cow every morning for a year. 'I find some of David Archer's sneering lines about organic farming stick in my throat,' he says, 'not to mention his mockery of long-haired Liberals who work in television – since that's precisely what I am!'

Born in 1953 Tim was educated at Harrow, the University of East Anglia, and the Bristol Old Vic Theatre School. His first film role was as Roger Moore's right-hand man in *North Sea Hijack* and he has also been seen in *Pirates of Penzance, Success is the best Revenge* and the Channel 4 film *Winter Flight*.

Theatre credits include the Edinburgh fringe, rep at Plymouth and Coventry, and the *Pirates of Penzance* at Drury Lane. 'The pinnacle of my theatrical career so far

Graham Blockey

Carole Boyd

was when I played the Pirate King for three weeks between Tim Curry and Oliver Tobias.'

On television Tim has paid his mortgage by being the Opal Fruits' scoutmaster and appearing 'guinless' but surrounded by beautiful girls, but he is best known for his role as Tom Lacey in the BBC serial 'By the Sword Divided'.

BALLARD BERKELEY (Colonel Danby) received his greatest promotion rather late in life, when he was elevated from being a major in 'Fawlty Towers' to being a colonel in The Archers. His own wartime career, in fact, was spent with the Metropolitan Police!

He has had a dazzling career in films, starring with Anna Neagle in *The Chinese Bungalow* back in the 1930s, and still going strong today with *The Holdcroft Covenant* and *Vacation 11* released in 1985. Notable film appearances have included parts in *Night Callers*, *Operation Diplomat* and *In Which We Serve*.

In the 1930s he starred and featured in West End plays including *Heartbreak House* and *The Ghost Train*, and made a personal success as Larry in *Love on the Dole*.

He has been in hundreds of television productions from 'Swizzlewick' and 'United' to recent guest appearances in the BBC's 'To the Manor Born', 'Hi de Hi', and 'Are You Being Served?'

GRAHAM BLOCKEY (Robert Snell) took a degree in Medicine and worked as a hospital doctor at St Mary's, Paddington, for two years before deciding to embark on a theatrical career and enrolling at the Bristol Old Vic Theatre School.

Since leaving Bristol in 1982 he has done a wide variety of work in radio, including a lead part in Peter Terson's *Letters to the Otter* and the part of Germanicus in *I, Claudius*. Television viewers have seen him in 'Sweetheart' on Anglia TV and in BBC 1's 'The Best Years of Your Life'.

In the theatre he has worked in London Fringe productions, at the Edinburgh Festival, and at the Everyman Theatre, Cheltenham.

He lives in London with his wife and baby girl.

CAROLE BOYD (Lynda Snell) won the BBC Radio Drama Award during her final year at Drama School. After six months with the Radio Drama Company she worked extensively in the theatre, playing roles like Martha in *Who's Afraid of Virginia Woolf?*, Sheila in *A Day in the Death of Joe Egg* and Amanda in *Private Lives*. While working with Alan Ayckbourn's company in Scarborough she played June in *Way Upstream*, which later went to Houston, Texas, for a two-month season.

She was not completely lost to radio, however, and spent four years playing Shirley Edwards in 'Waggoners' Walk'.

Nigel Caliburn

She can also be heard regularly on Radio 4 and World Service drama productions; the Marshall Cavendish cassette series 'Little Story Teller', and in radio and television commercial voice-overs. Since joining The Archers she has discovered a fascination for growing things, and is now a keen gardener.

MARGOT BOYD (Marjorie Antrobus) had the rare distinction while studying at RADA of taking part in a play being produced by Bernard Shaw, *Heartbreak House*, and that was only the start of a glittering theatrical career that has included many major West End productions. 'I was particularly lucky to play opposite A. E. Matthews, my favourite actor in comedy, in *The Manor at Northstead*,' she says. In 1953 she did a season at Stratford, and it was then that she did her first radio broadcast from the BBC's Birmingham studios. After that came the musicals *Divorce me, darling* and *Waiting in the Wings* by Noel Coward, the play she has enjoyed acting in most of all.

Television work has included 'Dixon of Dock Green' and in 1969 she was invited to join the BBC Drama Repertory Company.

'Since then radio has been my first love,' says Margot. It was while working on the rep in London that she was given a small one-off part in The Archers – and made such a success of it that Marjorie Antrobus was written into the programme as a permanent character.

NIGEL CALIBURN (Nigel Pargetter) is no stranger to serial drama having played office-assistant Greg in Channel 4's 'Brookside', a wine waiter in Granada's 'Coronation Street', and a doctor in Yorkshire Television's 'Emmerdale Farm'. Aged 33, Nigel comes from Birmingham and has had a varied career that has included acting with the Prospect Theatre Company and working as a salesman selling iron pads!

RICHARD CARRINGTON (The Rev. Richard Adamson) was offered his part in The Archers in 1973, and reluctantly turned it down. Producer Tony Shryane needed him in the studio at Pebble Mill on a Wednesday afternoon and again the following Monday. 'The trouble was that on the Saturday in between I was due to be married – in Pennsylvania!'

Airline timetables were hastily consulted, however, and it was found to be just possible to keep all three appointments – so a wedding in America was speedily followed by a honeymoon in Edgbaston.

His most vivid memory of life in Ambridge is of conducting Doris Archer's funeral – in a real church with a full congregation – just a week after the death of his own father. He also remembers marrying Christine and George Barford (in the studio this time) and watching Christine walk up the aisle with her wedding dress slung over the arm of a sound-effects man, who was rustling it skilfully for the microphone.

Nowadays Richard spends most of his time as a radio interviewer, travelling the world to meet writers and record conversations about their lives and work. Among those he has especially enjoyed meeting are Graham Greene, John Updike, Salman Rushdie, and Peter Ustinov. And he thinks he is extremely lucky that a lot of his work involves staying at home – with his American wife and their three sons – being paid to read books.

CHARLES COLLINGWOOD (Brian Aldridge) – 'I was born in Canada in 1943. My father was looking for someone to fight. He failed and we came back to England in 1944 and have been here ever since.' The young Charles Collingwood grew up in the country near Andover and then went to Sherborne School, where he shocked his house master by saying he wanted to be a night club pianist.

He did go to RADA, however, and embarked on a career as an actor. 'It took me six years to earn enough to pay tax,' he recalls. 'I did various ghastly jobs like cleaning and delivering boxes of fruit and veg. round Marble Arch.'

By 1973 he had worked with various repertory companies and was playing in *The Other Half Loves* with Penelope Keith at Greenwich. 'Shortly after that I met actress Judy Bennett, who was playing Shula in The Archers, and we recorded three children's puppet series together for ATV – 'Mumfire', 'Cloppa Castle', and 'The Munch Bunch' – and after we'd recorded 150 shows together we realized we were meant for each other and got married.'

When he's not working he's a passionate club cricketer, mostly with the stage cricket club, and a very keen gardener. He and Judy live in London, and their daughter Jane was born in 1979, when Charles was playing in *Dirty Linen* at the Arts Theatre as well as The Archers – which made it a very busy year!

Charles Collingwood

Sara Coward

SARA COWARD (Caroline Bone), despite playing super-Sloane Caroline, has no connection, to her knowledge, with any branch, major or minor, of the English aristocracy! She is, in fact, a grammar-school girl from south-east London who went on to Bristol University and managed to get an honours degree in Drama and English while acting non-stop for three years. After that, she returned to London to finish training at the Guildhall School, where she won the Carlton Hobbs award. That gave her an Equity card and a six-month contract with the BBC Drama Repertory Company.

She went on to work in television and a wide selection of provincial theatres before going into the West End for The Prospect Company in *A Month in the Country* ('Which was very good,' she says) and then at The Ambassadors Theatre in *Let The Good Stones Roll*, a musical about the lives and loves of The Rolling Stones ('Which was very, very bad!')

Sara has also co-written plays for the London Fringe, one of which was a study of prostitution through 2,000 years called *The Oldest Profession* which was seen at the Bath Festival and was recommissioned by the Open University. She has the distinction of having a chapter to herself in Clive Swift's book *The Performing World of the Actor*.

JAN COX (Hazel Woolley) feels that 'Hazel is a wonderful part for any actress to play. You could call her the J.R. of Ambridge – mad, bad, and generally upsetting!'

Jan trained as an actress for four years, and her career has been extraordinarily varied – from singing and dancing in a cabaret trio to community and children's theatre, working in churches and old people's homes. In her spare time she enjoys dancing, keep fit, writing poetry, yoga, and reading autobiographies.

'I got a few jibes from my friends when I started playing Hazel Woolley,' she says. 'Remarks like "Don't ever take her to a French restaurant, she eats the *chef* instead of the food!" I enjoy playing the part, though, and I'm sure there's some good in her. The trouble is, I haven't found it yet!'

Jan has played the part of Susan in BBC television's 'Juliet Bravo'.

PAMELA CRAIG (Betty Tucker) first appeared on the professional stage as Peter Pan at the Theatre Royal, Leicester, when she was fifteen. After that she went to the Birmingham Theatre School, where Alan Devereux was a fellow pupil. She has worked extensively in rep, and spent several years working in radio drama in Manchester and Leeds, doing plays by Alan Plater, Henry Livings, Trevor Griffiths, and Alan Ayckbourn – who was a radio producer himself at the time.

In the West End, Pamela was directed in Charles Wood's *Meals on Wheels* by John Osborne. Television appearances include episodes of 'Z Cars' and thirteen weeks in 'Coronation Street' as Jackie Marsh, a journalist who had an affair with Ken Barlow. Her most recent television appearance was in 'The Pickersgill Primitive' by Mike Stott.

In her private life Pamela is married to actor Terence Brook, who is still recognized (despite beard and spectacles) as the 'lonely man' of Strand cigarette adverts in the 1960s!

ANNE CULLEN (Carol Tregorran) studied at the Royal Academy of Music during the war and was later to become a sub-professor there under Rose Bruford, and to teach broadcasting techniques at the academy for fifteen years. She was an adjudicator for the Associated Board of the Royal Schools of Music, and has also been on the examining board for the LRAM diploma.

Her acting career began in 1945 when she won the Royal Academy's gold medal for acting, and was invited to join the BBC drama rep. After that came weekly rep in the theatre, and work in films and television, and an enormous variety of radio work, including two years with Radio Luxembourg in serials like 'Dan Dare'.

She joined The Archers in 1954 to play cool young businesswoman Carol Grey whose long, fraught romance with John Tregorran was to be one of the programme's best-remembered stories. She maintained her interest in the theatre, though, and played several lead parts at the Theatre Royal, Margate, with actor Monte Crick – who was the second Dan Archer.

RICHARD DERRINGTON (Mark Hebden) went straight into repertory after drama school – Birmingham, then Scarborough (with the Alan Ayckbourn Company), Salisbury, Nairobi, St Andrews and Liverpool – then, in 1975, he joined the Royal Shakespeare Company for three years and went to New York with the RSC's *Henry IV* and *Henry V*. After that he joined the Old Vic Company for their world tour of *Hamlet*.

Richard has been seen on television in programmes ranging from 'The New Avengers' to 'Pericles' and on radio he has played a host of classic parts – Feste, Puck, Charles Egremont in Disraeli's 'Sybil' and Oswald in 'Ghosts'.

In 1984 he gave the first performance of his one man show 'Taylor's Tickler', and since then it has been seen in theatres, pubs, and halls throughout England, and in June 1984 he played it for a week at the National Theatre. It has been recorded as a 'Play of the Week' by the BBC World Service, and in 1985 Richard was invited to take the play on an extensive tour of the United States.

Richard is married to Louise, who teaches the deaf and physically handicapped, and they live in a renovated cottage (surrounded by ducks and chickens) deep in the Gloucestershire countryside. Their son, Giles, was born in 1987.

ALAN DEVEREUX (Sid Perks) is a member of the only father/daughter partnership in the programme – his real-life daughter Tracy-Jane plays clever grammar-school girl Lucy Perks. Born in 1941, Alan went to school in Sutton Coldfield. When he was fourteen he started going to evening classes to study speech and drama, and a year later he went to the Birmingham Theatre School. BBC radio plays soon followed, and 'walk-on' parts in television, and he made his first professional stage appearance at Birmingham Rep in 1956. 'I spent five years in stage-management with Derek Salberg's repertory companies at the Alex in Birmingham and The Grand in Wolverhampton,' he recalls. 'Working as an ASM in weekly rep, and playing small parts, was a very thorough way to learn about the theatre.'

He has been playing the part of Sid Perks since 1962, and has also performed in over 100 radio plays, supplied 'voice-overs' to countless audio-visual films for industry, appeared in three television commercials, and voiced more than 6000 radio adverts.

Alison Dowling

ALISON DOWLING (Elizabeth Archer) – 'I wouldn't be playing Elizabeth,' says Alison Dowling, 'if I'd managed to achieve my first ambition in life – ballet. The trouble was I didn't develop into a sylph-like swan, I developed hips instead! So with my promising career ruined, my aspirations shattered, I was forced into retirement – undiscovered – at the age of eleven!'

Acting soon followed, though, with a pantomime audition in Shepherd's Bush leading to the offer of a place at the Barbara Speake Stage School, where she trained from 1972 to 1977. During this time she appeared in many BBC television plays including 'The Love School' and 'Grange Hill' and in 'Bless Me Father' and 'Quatermass' for Thames. She also worked for Ken Russell in two of his films – *Mahler* then *Tommy*. 'In *Tommy* I was young Tommy's voice and so far that's been my one and only disc.'

Since leaving theatre school Alison has been constantly busy in the theatre and in television – she played Jane Hardcastle in Yorkshire Television's 'Emmerdale Farm' – and in 1982 she went to America and toured with the Barn Theatre Company. She also works extensively in radio and television voice-overs, film dubbing, recording plays and stories, and foreign language tapes.

PATRICIA GALLIMORE (Pat Archer) was a successful radio actress right from the start, winning the BBC's radio drama competition while still at drama school in Birmingham, and going straight off to a six-month contract on the BBC rep in London. After that she was in demand for a wide variety of radio plays and serials, including 'Wuthering Heights', 'The Forsyte Saga', and 'War and Peace'. She has read several serialized books on radio, worked in Schools Radio, and for several years she was a presenter of the much-lamented 'Listen With Mother'.

She returned to Warwickshire in 1973, and now lives in Henley-in-Arden with her solicitor husband, Charles, her son Tom, and daughter Harriet. Apart from radio work she does films and television commercials and has been seen in television dramas including the BBC serial 'Spy Ship'.

She is, though, particularly well experienced in radio serials, having had a part in 'The Dales' and spent three years playing the part of Barbara in 'Waggoner's Walk'. She joined the cast of 'The Archers' as Pat Lewis in 1974, and became Mrs Tony Archer the same year.

CHRISS GITTINS (Walter Gabriel) was born in 1902, and spent his childhood summers before the First World War at a lonely cottage in the Shropshire countryside. 'I remember coming home tired and hungry from school, which was seven miles away, and having to draw water from a sixty-foot well. I was very small and I was terrified of letting the windlass handle slip.

'Then there were the wild nights when, with a hurricane lamp, I had to go out to the old two-seater privy at the top of the garden, scared to death of the noises of the night around me. Once a Jenny Wren was attracted by the light and flew in through the air vent, and finished up tangled in my curls.'

Chriss went to drama school in Wolverhampton, where he made an early stage appearance as an extra in *Julius Caesar* at the Grand Theatre. 'I was a soldier at the top of a flight of steps, and didn't realize the chap playing the Soothsayer was hiding behind me. When he leaped out shouting "Beware the Ides of March" I was so startled I tottered down the steps wildly clutching my banner. The audience was amused, but Julius Caesar wasn't.'

Chriss has been in numerous plays during fifty years of broadcasting, and he's been playing Walter Gabriel since 1953. 'The war years were probably the most varied,' he says, 'making documentaries about people from all walks of life.' He has been awarded an OBE and in 1984 was the subject of 'This Is Your Life' on Thames Television.

Patricia Gallimore

PATRICIA GREENE (Jill Archer) attended grammar school and studied at the Central School of Speech and Drama. She was one of the first actors to go to Eastern Europe after the war. 'There were newspaper headlines about it,' she recalls. ' "Actress flies behind Iron Curtain to play Cow" and that sort of thing.' After that she did a series of jobs, from being a bus conductress and waitress to being a model and a cook – and all the time she worked whenever she could in the theatre. 'In Wales once I even blacked up and went on stage as a coal miner!'

At one point she considered joining the Rank Organization as a 'starlet', but in the end she didn't sign the contract. Instead she concentrated on the theatre: the fringe in London with George Devine, and then Oxford Rep.

Then, in 1956, came The Archers, and a new field of acting altogether. 'I was so ignorant of radio techniques', says Paddy, 'that when the script called for Jill to throw coffee over Phil I actually drenched poor Norman Painting in prop water.'

Living at Marlow, Patricia Green has a son, Charles.

MOLLIE HARRIS (Martha Woodford) started her BBC career as a writer, jotting down the stories and yarns she heard during nine years working on farms in Oxfordshire during seedtime and harvest, and sending them to producer Paul Humphreys in Birmingham. 'They were used on a programme called "In the Country" which was introduced by Phil Drabble,' she says. In time some of her writings were accepted on other programmes, like 'Regional Extra' and 'The Countryside in the Seasons'.

After that Mollie wrote her first book, the highly acclaimed autobiography of her childhood, *A Kind of Magic*, and she has been writing books ever since.

'I took an audition for radio plays back in the 1960s,' she recalls, 'but it was only in 1970 that I was given the part of Martha in The Archers.

TREVOR HARRISON (Eddie Grundy) is a Stourbridge lad, like Chriss Gittins. He went to the Birmingham Theatre School and then worked in rep in Birmingham and Coventry as well as doing a schools tour with 'Theatre in Education'. After that came television, with appearances in 'Get Some In', 'Hazel' and 'Stig of the Dump', and he has recently been spotted drinking and chatting-up girls in an advert for Harp lager. Children know him from 'Jackanory Playhouse' and 'The Basil Brush Show' and for his reading of stories on Radio 4's 'Listening Corner'.

It was his characterisation of Eddie Grundy, though, that brought him dazzling fame, three record releases (the latest being 'Clarrie' on Foxy Records) and his very own fan club. It has also made him wary about coincidences.

'In one episode Eddie was kicked by a cow, and the night the episode was broadcast a herd of cows surrounded my car in a country lane and kicked it hard.

'On another occasion Eddie's van broke down in the programme, and the same day my own vehicle spluttered to a halt.

'The greatest coincidence, though, started at the White Bear hotel in Shipston-on-Stour, where *Radio Times* took publicity pictures of Clarrie and Eddie's wedding reception, pretending it was "The Bull", Ambridge – where Clarrie was the barmaid.

'A year later I went back to the White Bear for a fan-club reunion, started chatting to the barmaid Julia Cook, and now I'm married to her!'

Trevor and Julia live in Leamington, when they are not travelling round the country so that Trevor can close things down. 'Other actors get asked to open things,' he says, puzzled, 'but I keep being asked to close things, like a store in Oxford Street and a festival in Salisbury. It's funny, that.'

Trevor's most recent television role has been as Terry in Central Television's 'King's Oak'.

BRIAN HEWLETT (Neil Carter) is a keen photographer and bird watcher and cares deeply about conservation of the countryside and the preservation of wildlife. He spends his holidays – when time and money allow – exploring in Peru, visiting game parks in Kenya, and observing the rare mountain gorillas in Rwanda, and he returns to delight his friends in the theatre and the Pebble Mill studios with showings of his remarkable photographs.

Brian trained at the Rose Bruford College in Kent, and his first professional job in the theatre was as a walk-on and understudy in *Lock Up Your Daughters* at London's Mermaid Theatre. After completing *Great Expectations* at the Mermaid – his performance was favourably noticed by Harold Hobson – he left to play the title part in a nationwide tour of Brendan Behan's *The Hostage*.

'My first radio broadcast was in a play called *Frost* and I shared leading roles with Chriss Gittins,' he recalls. 'Little did I realise how much work I would be sharing with Chriss in the future!'

Brian has been in the BBC Drama Repertory Company three times, but has always accepted theatre work whenever he can. 'I've been the Dame several times in Christmas pantos, love taking part in musicals, and had a superbly enjoyable time at London's Cambridge Theatre playing Amos Hart in *Chicago*.'

He has also worked extensively in television – from 'Emergency Ward Ten' and 'Probation Officer' to the BBC production 'Trelawney of the Wells'. He joined The Archers as Brookfield's new farming apprentice in 1973.

Crawford Logan

EDWARD KELSEY (Joe Grundy) trained at the Royal Academy of Music, after leaving the RAF in 1951 and graduated as a teacher of speech and drama. He also won the Howard De Walden Gold Medal and was winner of the Carlton Hobbs radio award in its second year of existence. 'Since then radio has always been my first love,' he says, 'although I've been involved in most other branches of the acting profession.'

His first theatre work was in the tour of *Reluctant Heroes*, and that was followed by many years in rep, notably at Guildford. He has made many television appearances over the years, most recently as Inspector Buxton in 'Juliet Bravo' and Titus Price in 'Anna of the Five Towns'. As something quite different, he has also provided the voices of Baron Greenback and Col K in the cartoon series 'Dangermouse'!

CRAWFORD LOGAN (Matthew Thorogood) was born and bred in Scotland and came to London to train at the Webber-Douglas Academy of Dramatic Art.

He played Sgt. Trotter in the 1984–85 London cast of *The Mousetrap*, and other West End credits have included Tom Stoppard's *Dirty Linen* and *New-Foundland*. His most recent theatre engagement was at Greenwich, playing Capt. Fraser in *For King and Country*.

He has played numerous leading classical and contemporary roles in repertory theatres such as Windsor, Southampton, Perth and Pitlochry. At the Thorndike Theatre, Leatherhead, he took on the daunting task of playing all five male roles in a two-handed version of *La Ronde*.

He was a guest lead artist in an episode of BBC Scotland's 'End of the Line' series.

Fiona Mathieson

Other television credits have included well known series such as 'Dr Who' and 'Secret Army'.

He is a very familiar voice on BBC Radio having literally thousands of plays for adults and children to his credit. He is also a frequent reader of 'Morning Story' and was a regular character in the radio drama series 'Waggoner's Walk'.

Married with two children, he is a keen soccer fan and proud of the fact that he is the longest serving supporter of Stirling Albion Football Club.

CHARLOTTE MARTIN (Susan Horobin) was born in Fontainebleau, near Paris, where her father was working at NATO headquarters, and grew up at the family home in Solihull. At the age of three she started at dancing school; when she was nine she took the lead in *Babooshka*, a Christmas play, and at secondary school she was found in every play that was staged. After school she successfully auditioned for a place at the Birmingham Theatre School. 'I remember the day I was accepted. I was so elated I ran skipping down the streets of Birmingham with an enormous smile on my face, grinning madly at everybody.'

After drama school Charlotte appeared at Birmingham Rep as the maid in *The Importance of Being Earnest* and shortly after that she auditioned for The Archers.

'I still can't get over the way listeners are involved in the programme – when Susan had her baby I received several "congratulations" cards!'

FIONA MATHIESON (Clarrie Grundy) has worked with most of the major provincial companies, since beginning her career at the Mermaid Theatre, in roles as varied as Sally Bowles in *Cabaret* and Dr Scott in *Whose Life is it Anyway?*. She has spent long seasons with The Crucible, Sheffield, and with Alan Ayckbourne's company in Scarborough, where she played the lead in *Travelling Hopefully* by Ken Whitmore, a performance she repeated on radio. In London she has been seen at theatres like The Half Moon and The King's Head, and played the blonde bombshell in *Andy Capp* at The Aldwych.

Her radio work has spanned everything from singing on 'Midweek' to reading Woman's Hour serials, and many radio plays. On television, plays include 'Relative Strangers', 'Big Deal', and 'It Takes a Worried Man', but she is perhaps best remembered as the dual-personality French girl Felice in 'The Agatha Christie Hour' play 'The Fourth Man' which she recorded for Thames.

JACK MAY (Nelson Gabriel), says his education was 'excellent – somewhere between *Decline and Fall* by Evelyn Waugh and *Sorrell and Son* by Warwick Deeping'.

Born in Henley-on-Thames, he knew from the earliest age that he was destined for an extrovert career. 'Barrister,

Archbishop, Prime Minister (Pity about that – Mrs Thatcher could have been my Chancellor of the Exchequer) or THE THEATRE.'

He spent the War in India, came back and was a teacher for a year, then went to Merton College, Oxford. After that he got a job at the renowned Birmingham Rep and stayed there for four years – 'with the exception of Paul Scofield a longer stay than any other actor' – and was the first actor to play Henry, consecutively, in the three parts of Henry VI, which he did at the Old Vic in 1954.

Between 1955 and 1985 he has been employed, he says modestly, as 'a jobbing actor', a phrase that covers countless film roles, leading parts in the West End, twenty-five television serials, and hundreds of radio parts. He's been in both versions of *Goodbye Mr Chips* and is the only actor to have played both Julius Caesar and Octavius Caesar in a major production at the Old Vic.

Among what he calls the 'unusual or bizarre' parts he has taken on he lists a film called *Cat Girl*, which was later described by John Boulting as the worst film ever made, and the part of a Chilean torturer in a play by Brian Phelan for Amnesty International.

TERRY MOLLOY (Mike Tucker) was at a Playgoers Party in Darlington when a genteel old lady approached him and asked tentatively if he really did play Mike Tucker – this was in the days when Mike Tucker was an aggressive union man, standing up for the rights of agricultural workers. When he replied 'yes' she immediately started to hurl abuse at him, demanding to know how he *dared* to be so awful to poor Phil Archer. Then she hit him.

'Nowadays,' says Terry, 'if people ask me if I'm Terry Molloy I answer "Er, maybe . . ." '

Terry is also Davros, creator of the Daleks, in BBC television's 'Doctor Who' – and in a recent poll was voted third most evil creature in the Universe. But he has also played the lovable Toad in *Toad of Toad Hall* at Birmingham Rep!

Terry has done an immense amount of theatre work, including tours with the Cambridge Theatre Company and the Prospect Theatre Company and a national tour of *Godspell*, and on television he has been seen in programmes varying from 'Angels' to 'Birds of Prey' and 'Artemis 81'. On radio he has been in over 200 plays, and was voted 'Best Actor' in the Society of Authors radio awards for his performance as Boko in Ron Hutchinson's 'Risky City'.

Terry is married to Heather Barrett, who plays Dorothy Adamson in the Archers, and they live in Birmingham.

HEDLI NIKLAUS (Kathy Holland) studied drama at the University of California where a tutor made her stand in large, crowded halls declaiming her vowels – 'did you ever hear anything as pure as that?' – and where she learned the method school of acting by pretending to be a jelly and made jelly noises with the department's 'jelly congregation'. Back in England she took a more conventional degree in drama at Manchester University and started her professional acting career with Brian Way's touring Company in schools all over England and Scotland. Since then she has been in rep in Birmingham, Coventry, and Worcester, as well as Torquay, where she met her husband, actor Leon Tanner. She has been in many radio and television plays and presented the Tyne-Tees series 'Look-Out'.

Kathy Holland is Hedli's third character in The Archers. She entered the programme as Libby Jones, a milk recorder, then came back as the Home Farm au pair Eva Lenz. It was while she was playing Eva that she married her husband Leon for the second time – he was also in the programme playing village bobby PC Coverdale! She and Leon live in a cottage in Stratford's Old Town, with their son Nick and daughter Kate.

NORMAN PAINTING (Phil Archer) had his first broadcast in 1945, and he was first heard as Phil Archer on 29 May 1950, when The Archers was broadcast for a trial week in the BBC's Midland Region. He has played the part ever since, and is the only member of the cast to have been in the programme continuously throughout its thirty-five years.

Norman did not, however, set out in life to be an actor. He left school at fifteen and after three years as a student librarian worked his way through Birmingham University, graduating with first-class honours. He then did research at Christ Church, Oxford, and became a tutor in Anglo Saxon at Exeter College. During this time he was active in university drama, both as a director and performer, and in 1949 he joined the BBC as writer and producer.

Since then he has written literally hundreds of radio plays and documentaries, including nearly 1,200 Archers scripts under the pen-name Bruno Milna (for which he and Edward J. Mason received a Writer's Guild Award). He has also become a well-known television personality in the Midlands for his highly praised programmes about gardens, and a national radio personality with appearances on 'Midweek', 'Quote – Unquote', 'Stop the Week' and Radio 2's 'On the Air'.

In 1976 Norman was made an OBE for services to broadcasting, and the Royal Agricultural Society have made him their only life governor in recognition of his twenty-five years' service to agriculture in the United Kingdom. He lives in a south Warwickshire village and is a trustee of the Warwickshire and Coventry Historic Churches Trust, and a patron of the Tree Council.

On The Archers twenty-fifth anniversary, he wrote a highly successful book about the programme, *Forever Ambridge*, which was updated and republished for its thirtieth anniversary.

ARNOLD PETERS (Jack Woolley) began his broadcasting career with a 'Children's Hour' programme called 'Hastings of Bengal' in 1951, and has now clocked up over 3,000 radio programmes, 250 television appearances, and has been in several feature films. He started his acting career at the Royal Theatre, Northampton, after service in the RAF, and spent five years in weekly and fortnightly rep before starting to get work with the BBC. He was a member of the BBC drama company in Birmingham in the early 1950s, and in 1953 he joined The Archers to play Len Thomas – and when Len was written out, he played the vicar, the Rev. David Latimer – and after the demise of the Rev. Latimer, he took a break from Ambridge until 1980, when he returned as Jack Woolley.

Arnold still lives in the East Midlands, where he has written and directed several pantomimes, and directed musicals including Gilbert and Sullivan. He is married with one daughter, Caroline, who teaches ballet at a London Stage School. His hobbies include painting, dancing, and music, and he plays as a member of a folk dance band.

ANGELA PIPER (Jennifer Aldridge) unwittingly upset a listener who wrote very severely about her to Brian Aldridge, Home Farm, Ambridge: 'I know you do not realise it, but your wife Jennifer is secretly visiting London to read letters on BBC television's "Points of View". You must stop this. She is taking work away from a qualified person, and cannot possibly need the money.'

Actress Angela Piper ('Who says I don't need the money!') must have upset the above correspondent even more if he saw her in Yorkshire Television's 'Life Begins at Forty' and 'Third Time Lucky' – not to mention several television commercials, lots of film voice-overs, and a recent stage appearance at the Belgrade Theatre, Coventry.

Angela trained for the stage at the Royal Academy of Music, where she won the broadcasting prize. After that came the theatre, working as an ASM and playing juvenile leads, more radio work, and eventually the part of rebellious young schoolgirl Jennifer Archer.

Apart from her acting, Angela also adjudicates at Music and Drama festivals, gives poetry readings, opens fêtes up and down the country, and with her television announcer husband, Peter, is bringing up three children in a country house where they are all surrounded by dogs, cats, chickens, ducks, geese, a rabbit and a guinea pig.

GRAHAM ROBERTS (George Barford) is the only member of the cast to have played lawn tennis in the Wimbledon Qualifying Rounds (he also represented his county and the British Universities). Graham played soccer and cricket long after leaving school, rowed in the Henley Royal Regatta, and to cap it all was treasurer of his local Pony Club!

The theatre finally commanded his interest and after training at the Bristol Old Vic Theatre School he went into rep and then spent two years as Artistic Director of the Garrick Playhouse, Altrincham.

Graham was in the world première of Eric Linklater's *Breakspear in Gascony* at the Edinburgh Festival, the Royal Performance of Goldoni's *Venetian Twins* at Liverpool, and toured Italy for the Old Vic with Ben Jonson's *The Alchemist*.

Feature films include *This Sporting Life, A Taste of Honey*, and *A Touch of Brass* and his many television parts include P.C. Aitken in 'Z Cars'.

Moving to Scotland he spent seven years with Grampian Television as a presenter and writer and now that he lives in Yorkshire he works as a continuity announcer for Yorkshire Television.

Graham is married to soprano Yvonne Robert, and together they make several tours each year with a highly acclaimed programme of words and music.

LESLEY SAWEARD (Christine Archer) recalls how 'In 1953 I was working as a teacher when I met the late Denis Folwell, who played Jack Archer, and he remarked on how similar my voice was to that of Pamela Mant, the girl who was playing Christine Archer. I had been trained as an actress, so I jokingly said: "If she leaves, let me know!" little realising how that chance remark was to change the whole course of my life.'

Pamela Mant did leave the programme shortly afterwards, and Lesley was called to Birmingham for an audition. She got the part, and the voice match with Pamela was so complete that hardly anyone noticed the change. 'I've been playing Christine ever since,' says Lesley, 'apart from the years when my two children were born.'

Lesley has made many public appearances as 'Chris' over the years, and particularly remembers being given a standing ovation by members of the Women's Institute at the Albert Hall; and being very moved when a blind man presented her with the first thing he had made since losing his sight.

Apart from The Archers Lesley works on film commentaries, audio-visual presentations, and commercials for both radio and television.

Lesley Saweard

Pauline Seville

PAULINE SEVILLE (Mrs Perkins) trained at RADA and her first job was with the Manchester Repertory Company, where the leading man was Noel Johnson, the original Dick Barton. In 1943 she went into ENSA and toured all over Britain and later Germany. More repertory work followed at Leicester and Newcastle, and then with Hilton Edwards' Dublin Gate Theatre Company at the Vaudeville Theatre in London.

Radio work has included 'Children's Hour' plays and 'Guilty Party', which was written by Archers scriptwriters Edward J. Mason and Geoffrey Webb. The part of Mrs Perkins came Pauline's way after her BBC audition was heard by Godfrey Baseley.

Pauline has not only played Mrs Perkins from the earliest days of the programme, she has also taken the parts of Rita Flynne and a girl called Audrey, who used to clean for John Tregorran.

Married to a Leicester businessman she has two children, a son of 27 and a daughter of 25.

COLIN SKIPP (Tony Archer) started writing scripts with actor Victor Maddern while working as an office boy with the Rank Organization and he determined to earn his living from the theatre. 'Then my country called me,' he says, 'and I spent two years as a private in the Pay Corps.' His National Service was not without distinction, however, because he was one of a dozen privates selected to form a new 'Electronic Accounting Development Unit' – in other words to test out a thing called a computer. Released by the Army, Colin won a scholarship to RADA and kept himself in food and clothes by washing dishes at the Lyon's Corner House at Oxford Circus. 'I became hooked on washing-up,' he recalls, 'starting with all those messy dishes and ending up with everything clean, neat, and tidy. A perfect performance every time!' Colin still does the washing-up at his home in St Annes-on-Sea.

After winning the RADA fencing prize and the BBC drama student prize he went into rep and it was while doing a summer season at Guernsey in 1968 that he met his wife-to-be actress Lisa Davies.

By then he was also appearing in television serials like 'United' and 'The Newcomers', had been in the West End revival of *The Long and the Short and the Tall*, and had been heard playing a schoolboy in a radio play.

'I was asked to audition for sixteen-year-old Tony Archer, and although I was nearly thirty at the time I got the part.'

The age gap, he says, has led to some amusing experiences. 'When I got married in 1970 one newspaper confused my age with that of Tony Archer and reported that Lisa was marrying an eighteen-year-old actor. All her friends thought she was cradle-snatching.'

JUNE SPENCER (Peggy Archer) was born in Nottingham where she played Mustardseed in *A Midsummer-Night's Dream* at a very early age, and then went on to study music, dancing, and acting. She became an after-dinner entertainer, writing her own comedy material; and then went into the theatre and did a stint of weekly, twice-nightly rep. 'I decided there must be an easier way of earning a living than that,' she says, 'so in 1945 I went into radio, where I've been happily employed ever since!'

In the past forty years she has played in every conceivable type of radio programme – 'Children's Hour' and pantomime, plays in obscure verse, 'Dick Barton' and 'Mrs Dale's Diary' – and she even played the Virgin Mary once.

June was a founder member of The Archers cast, playing Dan and Doris's cockney ex-ATS daughter-in-law Peggy in the trial week broadcast in 1950, as well as in the first national episode on 1 January 1951, and she also doubled as the flighty Irish Girl Rita Flynne.

In 1943 she took a break when she and her husband adopted two children, but she was back in Ambridge a year later playing Rita Flynn and other parts, and she resumed playing Peggy in 1962 when Thelma Rogers left the programme.

Two books of her comedy sketches and a one-act play have been published, and she has also written a series of three satirical feature programmes which were produced by the BBC, and a number of 'Odd Odes' for Cyril Fletcher.

When she isn't at Pebble Mill, June lives in a village in Surrey where she spends a lot of time gardening, doing crosswords, bird watching, and reading.

DAVID VANN (Detective Sergeant Dave Barry) was born on 12 January 1951 – just eleven days after The Archers – and he confesses that as a teenager he rapidly acquired a taste for drinking beer at the Old Bull inn at Inkberrow, the pub on which The Bull in Ambridge is said to have been based.

'Other contact with Ambridge remained purely that of a listener until 1981 when Sgt Barry arrived at Borchester nick', he says. In the meantime, David filled his time studying for an English degree at the University of East Anglia (where he spent most of his time with the Dramatic Society) followed by training at LAMDA and finally a career as a professional actor.

Stage appearances include roles as varied as a punk Ugly Sister in pantomime, Squire Blackheart in *The Thwarting of Baron Bolligrew*, and Mr Brown in *The Adventures of Paddington Bear*. He has spent a season with the Chichester Festival Theatre and played in two productions at the National Theatre.

Television viewers have seen him in 'The Professionals'

and the play 'Easy Money' in the BBC Playhouse series, and he has played many varying roles in radio plays.

TRACY-JANE WHITE (Lucy Perks) is known to most people as T-J, and her father in real life, as well as in The Archers, is Alan Devereux! Now studying English and Drama at a college in Cheshire, Tracy-Jane has taken part in amateur dramatics at Sutton Coldfield and school productions of *The Mikado* and *Iolanthe*. She has also performed a comic sketch ('Written with great success,' she says, 'by a hidden talent – my dad!') in the Birmingham Youth Show at the Hippodrome Theatre.

Tracy-Jane is 21 and has created the part of Lucy Perks during the last 6 years. She says she particularly enjoys visiting country shows and opening fêtes jointly with her father.

June Spencer

David Vann

George Hart, who died in April 1987, played the part of Jethro Larkin for twenty years. He gave to the character many virtues that were his own, and listeners delighted to hear the authentic voice of the countryman. Jethro became one of the best-loved characters in the programme.

Of the Archers team George said: 'It's just like one big happy family, that's the great thing, that's what makes it go.'

CHRISTINE ARCHER

Lesley Saweard

PHILIP ARCHER

Norman Painting